WATER~ WALKING

Discovering and
Obeying Your Call to
Radical Discipleship

JOHN ORTBERG

ZONDERVAN®

Water-Walking

Copyright © 2019 by John Ortberg

Abridgement by John Sloan.

Requests for information should be addressed to:
Zondervan, *3900 Sparks Drive SE, Grand Rapids, Michigan 49546*

Print ISBN 978-0-310-63200-9
Ebook ISBN 978-0-310-63201-6

Derived from material previous published in *If You Want to Walk on Water, You've Got to Get
Out of the Boat.*

Printed in the United States of America

19 20 21 22 23 24 25 26 27 28 / LSC / 12 11 10 9 8 7 6 5 4 3 2 1

To Sam Reeves and Max DePree,
who have taught me so much about getting out of the boat

CONTENTS

And early in the morning he came walking toward them on the sea. But when the disciples saw him walking on the sea, they were terrified, saying, "It is a ghost!" And they cried out in fear. But immediately Jesus spoke to them and said, "Take heart, it is I; do not be afraid."

Peter answered him, "Lord, if it is you, command me to come to you on the water." He said, "Come." So Peter got out of the boat, started walking on the water, and came toward Jesus. But when he noticed the strong wind, he became frightened, and beginning to sink, he cried out, "Lord, save me!" Jesus immediately reached out his hand and caught him, saying to him, "You of little faith, why did you doubt?"

When they got into the boat, the wind ceased. And those in the boat worshiped him, saying, "Truly you are the Son of God."

MATTHEW 14:25–33

PREFACE

I want to invite you to go for a walk.

The Bible is, among other things, a list of unforgettable walks. The first one was taken by God himself, who, we are told, used to walk in the garden in the cool of the day. But as a general rule, God asked people to walk with him.

There was the hard walk that Abraham took with his son Isaac on the road to Moriah. There was the liberating walk Moses and the Israelites took through the path that was normally occupied by the Red Sea, and the frustrating walk that took them on the roundabout way of the desert for forty years. There was Joshua's triumphant walk around Jericho, the disciples' illuminating walk to Emmaus, Paul's interrupted walk to Damascus.

But perhaps the most unforgettable walk of all was taken by Peter the day he got out of a boat and walked on the water. It is unforgettable not so much because of where he was walking as what he was walking *on* and who he was walking *with*. In this book, let Peter's walk stand as an invitation to everyone who, like him, wants to step out in faith, who wants to experience something more of the power and presence of God. There is a consistent pattern in Scripture of what happens in a life that God wants to use and improve:

- There is always a call.
- There is always fear.
- There is always reassurance. God promises his presence.
- There is always a decision. Sometimes, as with Moses and Gideon, people say yes to God's call. Sometimes, as with the ten frightened spies or the rich young ruler who spoke with Jesus, they say no.
- There is always a changed life. Those who say no are changed too. They become a little harder, a little more resistant to his calling, a little more likely to say no the next time.

I believe that this pattern from Scripture continues today. Together with this book we are going to learn the skills essential to "water-walking": discerning God's call, transcending fear, risking faith, managing failure, trusting God. I want to invite you to go for a walk. On the water.

Just remember one thing: If you want to walk on water, you've got to get out of the boat.

"Lord, if it is you . . ."
MATTHEW 14:28

ON WATER-WALKING

> *It's not the critic who counts; not the man who points*
> *out how the strong man stumbles, or where the doer*
> *of deeds could have done better. The credit belongs to*
> *the man who is actually in the arena . . . who, at best,*
> *knows in the end the triumph of great achievement, and*
> *who, at the worst, if he fails, at least fails while daring*
> *greatly. So that his place will never be with those cold*
> *timid souls who know neither victory or defeat.*
> THEODORE ROOSEVELT

Some years ago my wife arranged for us to ride in a hot-air balloon as a birthday gift. We went to the field where the balloons ascended and got into a little basket with one other couple. We introduced ourselves and swapped vocational information. Then our pilot began the ascent. The day had just dawned—clear, crisp, cloudless. We could see the entire Canejo Valley, from craggy canyons to the Pacific Ocean. It was scenic, inspiring, and majestic.

But I also experienced one emotion I had not anticipated. Want to guess?

Fear.

I had always thought those baskets went about chest high, but this one only came up to our knees. One good lurch would be enough to throw someone over the side. So I held on with grim determination and white knuckles.

I looked over at my wife, who does not care for heights at all, and relaxed a bit, knowing there was someone in the basket more tense than I was. I could tell, because she would not move—at all. During part of our flight there was a horse ranch on the ground directly behind her. I pointed it out because she loves horses, and, without turning around or even pivoting her head, she simply rolled her eyes back as far as she could and said, "Yes, it's beautiful."

About this time I decided I'd like to get to know the kid who was flying this balloon. I realized that I could try to psyche myself up into believing everything would be fine, but the truth was we had placed our lives and destinies in the hands of the pilot. Everything depended on his character and competence.

I asked him what he did for a living and how he got started flying hot-air balloons. I was hoping for his former job to be one full of responsibilities—a neurosurgeon, perhaps, an astronaut who missed going up into space.

I knew we were in trouble when his response to me began, "Dude, it's like this...."

He did not even have a job! He mostly surfed.

He said the reason he got started flying hot-air balloons was that he had been driving around in his pickup when he'd had too much to drink, crashed the truck, and badly injured his brother. His brother still couldn't get around too well, so watching hot-air balloons gave him something to do.

"By the way," he added, "if things get a little choppy on the way down, don't be surprised. I've never flown this particular balloon before, and I'm not sure how it's going to handle the descent."

My wife looked over at me and said, "You mean to tell me we are a thousand feet up in the air with an unemployed surfer who started flying hot-air balloons because he got drunk, crashed a pickup, injured his brother, and has never been in this one before and doesn't know how to bring it down?"

Then the wife of the other couple looked at me and spoke—the only words either of them were to utter throughout the entire flight.

You're a pastor. Do something religious.

So I took an offering.

The great question at a moment like that is, *Can I trust the pilot?*

Because of this, I have found myself drawn for many years to the story of Peter getting out of the boat and walking on the water with Christ, his Pilot. And what goes into the making of a water-walker.

WATER-WALKERS RECOGNIZE GOD'S PRESENCE

Peter and his friends got into a little boat one afternoon to cross the Sea of Galilee. Jesus wanted to be alone, so they were boating without him. Peter didn't mind—he'd been on boats his whole life. He liked them.

But this time a storm blew in. Not a minor squall, either. The gospel of Matthew says the boat was "tormented" by the waves. It was so violent that the only thing the disciples could do was to keep the boat upright. They wished the sides were a little higher and the wood a little thicker. By 3:00 a.m. I would imagine the disciples weren't worried about making it to the other side—they just wanted to stay alive.

Then one of the disciples noticed a shadow moving toward them on the water. As it got closer, it became apparent that it was the figure of a human being—walking on the water.

Take a moment to let that image sink in. The disciples were in distress, and the very person who was able to help them was approaching them. Only he wasn't in the boat and the disciples didn't recognize him. Amazingly enough, being boatless didn't seem to slow Jesus down at all.

But the disciples were convinced he was a ghost, so they were terrified and cried out in fear. In hindsight, we may wonder how they could have failed to know it was Jesus. Who else would it be? Let's probe deeper for a moment. What was Jesus up to, walking around on the lake at three o'clock in the morning?

David Garland finds a clue in Mark's version of this story. Mark tells us that Jesus "intended to pass them by" on the water, but when they saw him walking on the lake, they thought it was a ghost. Why did Jesus want to "pass them by"? Did he decide to race them? Did he want to impress them with a really neat trick?

Garland points out that the verb *par-erchomai* ("to pass by") is used in the Greek translation of the Old Testament as a technical term to refer to a theophany—those defining moments when God made "striking and temporary appearances in the earthly realm to a select individual or group for the purpose of communicating a message."

God put Moses in a cleft in a rock so Moses could see "'while my glory *passes by*.'... The Lord passed before him."

God told Elijah to stand on the mountain "for the Lord is about to *pass by*."

There is a pattern to these stories. In each case God had to get people's attention—through a burning bush, or wind and fire, or walking on the water. With each person God was going to call them to do something extraordinary. In each situation the person that God called felt afraid. But every time that people said "yes" to their calling, they experienced the power of God in their lives.

So when Jesus came to the disciples on the water intending "to pass them by," he was not just doing a neat magic trick. He was revealing his divine presence and power. *You can trust me. You know my character and my competence. You can safely place your destiny in my hand. Take courage. It's me.*

They didn't fully grasp it yet, but God was visiting them in the water-walking flesh.

Matthew wants his readers to know that Jesus often comes when least expected—3:00 a.m., in the middle of a storm. Dale Bruner notes that, "according to the Holy Scriptures, human extremity is the frequent meeting place with God." Those divinely appointed defining moments will come to you and me. He still asks his followers to do extraordinary things. And if you're not looking for him, you just might miss him.

We don't know how eleven in the boat responded to that voice. Perhaps with confusion, wonder, disbelief, or a little bit of each.

But one of them, Peter, was about to become a water-walker. He recognized that God was present—even in the most unlikely place. He realized that this was an extraordinary opportunity for spiritual adventure and growth. So he got an idea.

He decided to do something religious.

WATER-WALKERS DISCERN BETWEEN FAITH AND FOOLISHNESS

Peter blurted out to the water-walker, "If it is you, command me to come to you on the water." This is not just a story about risk-taking; it is primarily a story about *obedience*. That means I will have to discern between an authentic call from God and what might simply be a foolish impulse on my part.

Matthew is not glorifying risk-taking for its own sake. Jesus is not looking for bungee jumping, hang-gliding, day-trading, tornado-chasing Pinto drivers. This is not a story about extreme sports. It's about *extreme discipleship*. This means that before Peter gets out of the boat, he had better make sure Jesus thinks it's a good idea. So he asks for clarity, "If it is you, command me...."

Peter had enough faith to believe that he too could share the adventure. He decided he wanted to be part of history's original water-walk. *Command me.*

WATER-WALKERS GET OUT OF THE BOAT

Before we go any further, I want you to put yourself in the story. Picture in your mind how violent the storm must have been if it was strong enough to keep seasoned professionals struggling just to avoid being capsized.

The water is rough. The waves are high. The wind is strong. There's a storm out there. And if you get out of the boat—whatever your boat might happen to be—there's a good chance you might sink.

But if you don't get out of the boat, there's a guaranteed certainty that you will never walk on the water. I believe there is something—Someone—inside us who tells us there is more to life than sitting in the boat. You were made for something more than merely avoiding failure. So let me ask you a very important question: *What's your boat?*

Want to know what your boat is? Your fear will tell you. Just ask yourself this: *What is it that most produces fear in me— especially when I think of leaving it behind and stepping out in faith?*

For David, it is his vocation. He has been a builder for thirty-five years; he is in his late fifties now. But he has been gnawed his whole life by a sense that God was calling him into church ministry. He has quieted his conscience by giving away a lot of money and doing many good things, but he can't shake off the haunting fear that he has missed his calling. And he's afraid that perhaps it's too late.

For Kathy, it is a relationship. She has been involved for years with a man whose commitment to her is ambivalent at best. He is sending her signals that everyone else can read clearly; he never initiates the language of affection, avoids talking about their future, and creates as much distance from her as possible. But she never pursues discovering his true feelings—she's too frightened.

Maybe your boat is success. That was the case for the rich young ruler in the Bible. Jesus asked him to get out of the boat ("sell all that you have, give the money to the poor, and come and follow me") but he decided not to. He had a very nice boat. A yacht. It handled well, and he liked it too much to give it up.

What is your boat? In what area of your life are you shrinking back from fully and courageously trusting God? Fear will tell you what your boat is. Leaving it may be the hardest thing you ever do.

But if you want to walk on the water, you've got to get out of the boat.

WATER-WALKERS EXPECT PROBLEMS

So Peter goes to the side of the boat. The other disciples are watching closely. They have seen Peter shoot off his mouth before—a lot. They wonder how far he'll take this thing.

He puts one foot over the side, carefully gripping the edge of the boat. Then the other foot. He's holding on with grim determination and white knuckles.

Then he does something religious—he lets go. He abandons himself utterly to the power of Jesus. And suddenly, for the first time in history, an ordinary human being is walking on the water.

Then it happens. Peter "saw the wind."

Reality sets in, and Peter asks himself, *What was I thinking?* He realized he was on the water in the middle of a storm with no boat beneath him—and he was terrified. The storm should have come as no surprise—it's been there all along. What has really taken place is that Peter's focus has shifted from the Savior to the storm.

We all know what it is to "see the wind." You begin a new adventure full of hope. Maybe it's a new job; maybe you're testing an area of spiritual giftedness; maybe you're trying to serve God in a new way. At the beginning you are full of faith—it's blue skies.

Then reality sets in. Setbacks. Opposition. Unexpected obstacles. You see the wind. It should be expected—the world's a pretty stormy place. But somehow trouble still has the power to catch us by surprise.

Because of the wind, some people decide never to leave the boat. If you get out of the boat, you will face the wind and the storm out there. But you might as well know now, there is no guarantee that life in the boat is going to be any safer.

If you step up to the plate, you may strike out. The greatest hitters in the world fail two times out of three.

But it you don't step up to the plate, you will never know the glory of what it is to hit a home run. There is danger in getting out of the boat. But there is danger in staying in it as well. If you live in the boat—whatever your boat happens to be—you will eventually die of boredom and stagnation. *Everything is risky.*

WATER-WALKERS ACCEPT FEAR AS THE PRICE OF GROWTH

Now we come to a part of the story you may not like very much. I don't care for it much myself. The choice to follow Jesus—the choice to grow—is the choice for the constant recurrence of fear. You've got to get out of the boat a little every day.

Let me explain. The disciples get into the boat, face the storm, see the water-walker, and are afraid. "Don't be afraid," Jesus says. Peter then girds up his loins, asks permission to go overboard, sees the wind, and is afraid all over again. "Don't be afraid," Jesus says.

Here is a deep truth about water-walking: *The fear will never go away.* Why? Because each time I want to grow, it will involve going into new territory, taking on new challenges. And each time I do that, I will experience fear again. As Susan Jeffers writes, "The fear will never go away, as long as I continue to grow."

Never! Isn't that great news? Now you can give up trying to make fear go away. It's a package deal. The decision to grow always involves a choice between risk and comfort. This means that to be a follower of Jesus you must renounce comfort as the ultimate value of your life. Would you like to guess the name of the best-selling chair in America?

La-Z-Boy.

Not Risk-E-Boy.

Not Work-R-Boy.

La-Z-Boy. We want to immerse ourselves in comfort. We have developed a whole language around this. People say, "I want to go home and *veg out*—make myself as much like vegetation as humanly possible, preferably in front of a television set."

We have a name for people who do this in front of TV, too: couch potatoes. Couch potatoes in their La-Z-Boys.

The eleven disciples could be called "boat potatoes." They didn't mind watching, but they didn't want to *do* anything.

And as we will see in this book, both choices—risk and comfort—tend to grow into a habit. Each time you get out of the boat, you become a little more likely to get out the next time. It's not that the fear goes away, but that you get used to living with fear. You realize that it does not have the power to destroy you.

On the other hand, every time you resist that voice, every time you choose to stay in the boat rather than heed its call, the voice gets a little quieter in you. Then at last you don't hear its call at all.

WATER-WALKERS MASTER FAILURE MANAGEMENT

As a result of seeing the wind and giving in to fear, Peter began to sink into the water. So here is the question: Did Peter fail?

Failure is not an event, but rather a *judgment* about an event. Failure is not something that happens to us or a label we attach to things. It is a way we think about outcomes.

Before Jonas Salk developed a vaccine for polio that finally worked, he tried two hundred unsuccessful ones. Somebody asked him, "How did it feel to fail two hundred times?"

"I never failed two hundred times in my life," Salk replied. "I was taught not to use the word 'failure.' I just discovered two hundred ways how not to vaccinate for polio."

Somebody once asked Winston Churchill what most prepared him to risk political suicide by speaking out against Hitler during the years of appeasement in the mid–1930s, then to lead Great Britain against Nazi Germany. Churchill said it was the time he had to repeat a grade in elementary school.

"You mean you failed a year in grade school?" he was asked.

"I never failed anything in my life. I was given a second opportunity to get it right."

Jonas Salk made two hundred unsuccessful attempts to create a polio vaccine. *Was Jonas Salk a failure?*

Winston Churchill repeated a grade in elementary school. *Was Winston Churchill a failure?*

Did Peter fail?

Well, I suppose in a way he did. His faith wasn't strong enough. His doubts were stronger. "He saw the wind." He took his eyes off of where they should have been. He sank. He failed.

But here is what I think. *I think there were eleven bigger failures sitting in the boat.*

Once you walk on the water, you never forget it—not for the rest of your life. I think Peter carried that joyous moment with him to his grave.

And only Peter knew the glory of being lifted up by Jesus

in a moment of desperate need. Peter knew, in a way the others could not, that when he sank, Jesus would be wholly adequate to save him. He had a shared moment, a shared connection, a shared trust in Jesus that none of the others had.

WATER-WALKERS SEE FAILURE AS AN OPPORTUNITY TO GROW

As soon as Peter asks for help, Jesus is there. He helps Peter physically by pulling him from the water. But he also helps Peter grow by pinpointing the problem: "You of little faith, why did you doubt?"

I don't think Jesus is being harsh or critical here.

The problem was quite clear: Whether Peter sank or water-walked depended on whether he focused on the storm or on Jesus. But now he understood his dependence on faith much more deeply than he would have if he had never left the boat. It was his willingness to risk failure that helped him to grow.

Even more than we hate to fail, we hate for other people to see us fail. If I had been Peter, I would have been tempted to try to cover up what happened when I got back into the boat with the other disciples

Sir Edmund Hillary made several unsuccessful attempts at scaling Mount Everest before he finally succeeded. After one attempt he stood at the base of the giant mountain and shook his fist at it. "I'll defeat you yet," he said in defiance. "Because you're as big as you're going to get—*but I'm still growing.*"

Every time Hillary climbed, he failed. And every time he failed, he learned. And every time he learned, he grew and tried again. And one day he didn't fail.

WATER-WALKERS LEARN TO WAIT ON THE LORD

This story about risk is also a story about waiting. The disciples had to wait in the storm until the fourth watch of the night. Why couldn't Jesus have made the wind die down *before* Peter got out of the boat?

Maybe because they—like us—needed to learn something about waiting.

We have to learn to wait on the Lord to receive power to walk on the water. We have to wait for the Lord to make the storm disappear.

In some ways, "waiting on the Lord" is the hardest part of trusting. It is not the same as "waiting around." It is putting yourself with utter vulnerability in his hands.

All my life I have loved to talk. When I was not yet two years old, I memorized my sister's part in a Sunday school pageant and demanded to be allowed to say it as well. (So I'm told; I don't personally remember this at all.) In surveys, fear of public speaking is consistently named as most peoples' number one fear—even ahead of death. I never understood this, because early in life it became a source of joy to me.

When I first began to preach and teach, I found it a

deeply moving experience. I had some sense that this is what I was made to do. It was part of my calling in my ministry.

One Sunday early on, I was about ten minutes into the message when I started getting very warm and dizzy. The next thing I knew, I was lying on the ground with several anxious faces checking to see if I was all right. I had fainted in the middle of a sermon.

After a year of studying abroad, I returned to the same church. The very next time I went to preach, the same thing happened. I went down ten minutes into the talk.

And unfortunately for me, this was a Baptist church, not a charismatic one. It wasn't the kind of church where you get credit for this sort of thing. No one interpreted it as being "slain in the Spirit." When you're a Baptist, fainting is just fainting. It did increase attendance for a while, somewhat like the possibility of an accident at the Indy 500—people don't exactly hope that one will happen, but they don't want to miss it if it does.

Well-meaning people offered all kinds of advice: "You just need to try really hard to relax and trust more." Ever try *really hard* to relax?

I was scheduled to preach quite often that summer. The senior pastor of the church, who was on sabbatical, offered to take me off the hook by getting some replacements.

But somehow I knew that if I didn't get up and speak that next weekend, it wasn't going to get any easier. I asked God to take away the fear of its happening again. He didn't. I remembered the passage from Isaiah—

> Even youths will faint and be weary,
>> and the young will fall exhausted;
> but those who wait for the Lord
>> shall renew their strength.

So I got up and preached. Not a great sermon by any stretch of the imagination, although the congregation was alarmingly attentive. It was nothing dramatic; it is done every Sunday by thousands of men and women around the world. But I made it to the end, which was a personal triumph.

If I don't preach, I will never again know the exhilaration of doing what I believe God has called me to do. I will not be faithful to what I understand to be my calling. So I am learning to wait.

WATER-WALKING BRINGS A DEEPER CONNECTION WITH GOD

Jesus is still looking for people who will get out of the boat. Why risk it? I believe there are many reasons:

- It is the only way to real growth.
- It is the way true faith develops.
- It is the alternative to boredom and stagnation that causes people to wither up and die.
- It is part of discovering and obeying your calling.

I believe there are many good reasons to get out of the boat. But there is one that trumps them all: *The water is where Jesus is.* Because Peter did this, both he and his friends came to a deeper understanding of their Master than ever before. They came to see more than ever that they could place their destinies in his hands with confidence. They understood that the One in their boat was the One alone who treads the waves of the seas—and they worshiped him.

How about you? When was the last time you got out of the boat?

Maybe there was a time in your life when you were walking on the water on a regular basis. A time when your heart was much like Peter's: "Command me. Tell me to come to you." A time when you would risk sharing your faith even if it meant rejection; giving, even if it meant sacrifice; serving, even if it meant the possibility of failure. Sometimes you sank. Sometimes you soared. But you lived on the edge of faith.

But if you get out of the boat, I believe two things will happen. The first is that when you fail—and you will fail sometimes—Jesus will be there to pick you up. And the other thing is, every once in a while you will walk on the water.

So Peter got out of the boat, started walking
on the water, and came toward Jesus.
MATTHEW 14:29

BOAT POTATOES

*The dismal company whose lives knew neither praise
nor infamy; who against God rebelled not, nor to Him
were faithful, but to self alone were true.*
DANTE ALIGHIERI

Anytime a gift is given, the recipient must choose to respond in one of two ways. The first way says, *This gift is so valuable it can't be risked.* Those who follow the first way realize that when the gift is brought out of the box and into the open, things may not always go well. The gift may be poorly used sometimes. It may not always be admired by others the way we want. It may even get broken. Taking the gift out of the box is always a risk.

The second way says, *This gift is so valuable it must be risked.* Those who follow the second way understand that if the gift is not brought out of the box, it will never be used at all. To leave the gift in the box is to thwart the desire of the giver. *There is no tragedy like the tragedy of the unopened gift.*

You, too, have been given a gift. We will look in the next chapter at how to discover what's inside your box—how to discern what God has gifted you and called you to do. But for now I want to invite you to do a bit of ruthless self-assessment. Along with the gift you have been given a choice—whether or not you will open and use what was given to you. Is your life following the first way or the second?

Peter chose the second way. Dale Bruner writes, "It is important to see that Peter did not ask Jesus for a *promise*—e.g., 'Lord, promise me I won't sink'—but specifically for a *command:* 'Lord, if it is you, *command* me.'" Peter didn't ask for a guarantee, just an opportunity.

The disciples who stayed in the boat were followers of the first way. They did not want to risk brokenness or failure. They treasured safety over growth. The Lord wanted to "pass them by"—to reveal himself in his adventuresome splendor—not to bypass them! The ultimate adventure of faith was something they were content to watch from the sidelines. They didn't want to be passed by, just passed up. Let them stand for all who ask not for a command but a promise, who seek not a mission but a guarantee.

They understood the cost of getting out of the boat. They were very much aware of the pain of potential failure, embarrassment, inadequacy, criticism, and perhaps even loss of life.

But what they were not so aware of was another price—the cost of staying in the boat.

The High Cost of Being
a Boat Potato

If I had to name, in a single word, the price you pay for being a boat potato, I think the word written on the price tag would read *growth*.

Think about the excitement of parents whose child says his first word. Yesterday he could only cry or babble—today he has joined the ranks of those who speak. His parents are excited.

Consider the sense of fulfillment in the leaders of a company that is expanding, achieving its mission, giving vocational opportunities to men and women who yesterday didn't have any. They are watching the miracle of *growth*.

On the other hand, there are few things sadder than stagnation.

Not many people plan a vacation to the Dead Sea.

Watch a marriage that was begun with hope and dreams, but has now plateaued, where affections have cooled and intimacy has faded. Rather than name the problem, face their pain, and ask for help, the couple resign themselves to a life of mediocrity, living together as intimate strangers.

This is a way that leads to stagnation—unrealized potential, unfilled longings. It leads to a sense that I'm not living *my* life; the one I was supposed to live. It leads to boredom.

There is no tragedy like the tragedy of the unopened gift:

It's as if I've lived half my life waiting for life to begin, thinking it's somewhere off in the future. As Thoreau hauntingly put it, "I did not wish to live what was not life.... I wanted to live deep and suck out all the marrow of life."

21

To serve as a wake-up call to potential boat potatoes, Jesus once told a story about a CEO and his three employees. Each of them was given a lavish opportunity. Like Peter. Like you and me. The Lord "intended to pass them by." Each of them had to decide what they would do.

Jesus teaches us three principles about the master—about God and the opportunity he offers us—we must understand if we are to embrace his gift.

HE IS THE LORD OF THE GIFT

In those days there were no corporations as we know them. When the psalmist said, "Lift up your heads, O ye Gates," he wasn't thinking of Bill. Wealth was concentrated in a few rich households.

This is the story about one of them. The master gathers together three key employees and "entrusted his property to them."

Jesus talks about vast sums of money. The master gives his first servant five talents, the second servant two, and the third one. A talent was an expression for a sum of money worth in the neighborhood of fifteen years' wages. In that era, people lived from day to day, and to have accumulated one year's worth of wages was enormous wealth.

As Kenneth Bailey writes in his great treatment of this parable, *Poet and Peasant*, it dawns on this first servant that this is an unbelievable opportunity. This is a chance for all of them to exercise initiative, use judgment, test their skills in the marketplace, and potentially rise to positions of greater responsibility. Most likely there would have been an implicit arrangement for them to share in profits as well.

Jesus tells the story of the talents because the lord of the gift offers the chance of a lifetime. Up until now, the servants have simply been carrying out somebody else's orders. Their lives have been routine, predictable, and safe. They have had little authority, few resources, and limited responsibility. Then, with a single act, the master changes their destinies forever. If we were to listen to the first servant, he might say something like this:

I thought my whole life was condemned to be routine. I had dreams, but couldn't pursue them; passions, but couldn't follow them; talents, but couldn't test them. I was never in a position to plan, take risks, or take initiative. My life was comfortable. I wasn't facing starvation, but I longed for something more. I wanted to make a difference.

And just when I was ready to give up hope, the master did something I've never heard of anyone doing before. He called me into his office, looked at me from behind his desk with a twinkle in his eye, and entrusted a large portion of what belongs to him to me. I can't believe he has that kind of faith in me. I can't believe I have this opportunity. I feel like a thoroughbred that's been set free to run.

The first servant realizes he has just been offered the chance of a lifetime. This explains a very important detail in this story, namely, why Jesus says the first employee responded "at once." The employee realizes it would be insane to let anything interfere. He responds at once because the thought of losing the chance of a lifetime is intolerable.

He responds at once because if someone offers you a front row seat on the NASDAQ in a bull market, you don't ask them if maybe they were thinking about somebody else.

"At once" isn't so much a chronological detail as a statement about the recognition of reality. The first servant realizes that as long as he lives, he will never have another chance like this. He will not be sidetracked or distracted. Jesus says this is how it is with anyone who grasps what God offers.

In place of the word *talent*, you might think about your life.

Your mind. Your abilities. Your spiritual gifts. Your body. Your money. Your will.

In fact, we get the meaning of the word *talent* from this very story. He has been very generous, the lord of the gift. He offers us himself as the best gift of all.

All human beings, including you and me, give their lives to something. Between this day and your last day, you will give your life to something. The only question is, what will you give your life to? Will it be worthy?

Let me get more personal: You had better respond *at once*.

The opportunity to use whatever gifts you have in the service of the Lord of the Gift is the chance of a lifetime. But it will slip away from you unless you are very intentional. The time to respond is *at once*.

But the third servant fails to do this. He takes the greatest gift he will ever be given and buries it in a field. Why would he do such a thing? What would cause a human being to discard the chance of a lifetime?

HE IS THE LORD OF THE SETTLED ACCOUNT

This brings us to a second truth about the master. Somehow the third servant forgets a very important fact of life. He forgets that the lord of the gift is coming back. But the day comes. "After a long time, the master of those slaves came back and *settled accounts* with them."

There is an odd tendency in human beings to think we can worm or charm our way out of the consequences of our actions. Have you ever tried to finesse a police officer out of a traffic ticket? *(Honest, officer, I thought the speedometer was broken.)* Ever try to bluff your way with a lame excuse for being late to a teacher, boss, or spouse? This is a tendency that starts early in life.

It is amazing to me how often we forget this. So many people blame their refusal to get out of the boat on some external circumstance:

- I would develop my gifts more thoroughly, but I have a boss who stifles my initiative.
- I would pursue another job, but I need the money/security/familiarity of this one.
- I would devote myself more fully to spiritual growth, but I can't find the time.

I have been given a gift. It may not look like much—but it's mine. It's all I have. It was given to *me*.

The master is coming back. He's going to settle up—with all the CEOs, presidents, prime ministers, network anchors, mothers and fathers, plumbers, teachers, and you and me.

And he will ask, What did you do with what I gave you?

He will not ask your boss about this, or your spouse, or your parents, or friends—he will ask you.

A performance review is coming my way that will make every other performance review I've ever been through look pretty inconsequential. This is what the third servant forgot, which enabled him to justify—at least to himself— burying his gift with so little concern.

THE SETTLED ACCOUNT: A COMPARISON

In this story there are two variables. First, there are varying amounts of gifts. One man gets five, another two, a third gets one. In this detail I think Jesus is simply reflecting life as we experience it. Some people are gifted in ways that will be visible and celebrated in this world; others are gifted in ways that remain quiet and unseen.

The variable that does matter is what each servant does with what he's been given. Here there are three servants because Jesus wants to make it painstakingly clear that the size of the gift is not the crucial variable. Even though the first servant receives a gift much larger than the second, the master responds in identical fashion to each of them. Jesus wants us to understand that the visible level of giftedness and calling is not the hinge point. Whether I'm a five-talent, two-talent, or one-talent person is not what counts in the long run.

I must ruthlessly refuse to compare my talents with anyone else.

Comparison will lead to pride and a false sense of

superiority if I'm ahead of someone, and misery if I'm behind. Or worse, I will discount and bury the irreplaceable treasure that the Lord of the Gift has given to me alone.

At the end of the day, God will not ask you why you didn't lead someone else's life or invest someone else's gifts. He will not ask, *What did you do with what you didn't have?*

Though, he will ask, *What did you do with what you had?*

Comparison is not an adequate excuse for the tragedy of an unopened gift.

When the lord of the settled account came to the third servant, he gave another rationale for his passivity: "For I knew that you were a hard man, reaping where you do not sow, and I was *afraid,* so I hid what you gave me." He wanted a promise that nothing would go wrong, not a command to do what's right.

Fear makes people bury the treasure God has given them. I hoard possessions because I am afraid I'll be bored or insecure if I don't have a lot of stuff. Fear of being poor is what made Jacob deceive his father.

I am afraid of what will happen if I tell the truth. Fear prompts me to lie. And it's not just deceit. When people are gossiping, I join in even though I know it's wrong because I am afraid of being left out.

Fear made the Israelites in the wilderness slight God's calling and care and clamor to return to Egypt.

Fear makes people disobedient to the calling of the master.

And what made Peter deny Jesus three times? Fear made these disciples betray their deepest value to their best friend at his hour of greatest need.

Look at most sin—yours and mine—and underneath it you will find fear.

In Scripture, when God calls Moses, Joshua, Gideon, or Esther to do something great for him, the single greatest obstacle that stands in the way is *fear*.

But we find a major surprise here. When the servant says fear of the master inhibited him, the master doesn't contradict him. The master does not say, *You have misunderstood me! Whether you use your gift or waste it doesn't really matter to me. I see this is painful for you, and my primary goal for you is to spare you pain—I'm so sorry I brought it up. Let's bury the whole issue.*

The master graciously lets pass the slur on his character. He doesn't remind the servant how generous he was in first place—that he had given this servant the chance of a lifetime. He says,

You got this much right: it matters to me. Your life—what you do with what I gave you—is a matter of supreme importance.

If that's really what you thought, at least you should have done something. You could have invested the money and gotten interest.

Jesus is pointing out that this rationale is just a smoke screen and not a serious reason for his action. This guy is simply trying to finesse his way out of a ticket. But that will not happen, because the master is the lord of the settled account; he cannot be finessed.

Fear is not an adequate excuse for the tragedy of an unopened gift.

One of the most sobering aspects of the story is that the servant is judged, not for doing *bad* things, but for doing *nothing.* He didn't steal or embezzle or defraud. He merely buried his gift.

Jesus uses two very serious words to describe him: wicked and lazy. We don't use these two words together much anymore. Nowadays hardly anyone would admit to laziness.

When someone is asked in a job interview about personal weaknesses, what is inevitably the answer? *I push myself too hard. My standards are too high. I expect too much of myself—work, work, work.* When is last time you heard someone say, *My problem is that I'm just too lazy. I can sit on the sofa, eat bonbons, and watch game shows by the month.*

Sloth as a spiritual sin is not the same thing as physical laziness. It can co-exist with much busyness. At its core, sloth consists of "loss of meaning, purpose, and hope, coupled with indifference to the welfare of others." It is the opposite of zeal and joy in the service of God.

Max DePree writes that unrealized potential is a sin—a very serious sin. This is a story about the sin of unrealized potential—the tragedy of the unopened gift. This is why one of the great temptations most of us face that could block us from getting out of the boat is comfort. You want to see how devoted we are to comfort? Walk into the average American home and hide the remote control, and watch what happens. Life without the remote control is an unbearable burden for the average American family. Then someone invented a TV with a beeper so that when you clap your hands, the remote control will beep until you find it.

What's most depressing about all this is that I know some people will read this chapter and the only thing they will take away from it is, *I gotta get one of those TVs with a beeper for the remote.*

When teachers want students to grow, they don't give them answers—they give them problems! *("If a train leaves Cleveland at 3:00 going 50 m.p.h....")* It is only in the process of accepting and solving problems that our ability to think creatively is enhanced, our persistence is strengthened, and our self-confidence is deepened. If someone gives me the answers, I may get a good score on a test, but I will not have grown. Just as our bodies simply will not grow stronger without being challenged to the point of exertion, so it is with our mind and spirit.

Comfort is not an adequate excuse for an unopened gift.

The Settled Account: Which Way Are You Following?

I want to ask you to exercise your imagination for a moment. Imagine that your life is over, and you are led to a small room. There are two chairs in the room, one for you and one for God (who gets a very large chair), and there's a VCR. God puts a tape into the machine. It has your name on it and is labeled *What Might Have Been.*

Imagine seeing what he might have done with your financial resources if you had trusted him to be generous. Imagine seeing what he might have done with your giftedness if you had trusted him enough to be daring. Imagine what he might have done in your relationships if you had trusted him enough to be fully truthful and fully loving. Imagine what he might have done with your character, if you had dared to confess sin, acknowledge temptation, and pursue growth.

But I also know that I want my life to come as close as I

can to realizing the goodness God intended for it. I know this is my only chance, and I know I want to minimize the gap between what shall be and what might have been as much as I can. I know that as long as I'm living, it's not too late—because I have this day. I know I want to ask God for commands, not guarantees, because when God commands, he enables. And I know that one day it will have been worth it.

HE IS THE LORD OF THE REWARD

There is one last truth about the master Jesus wants us to understand. The Lord of the Gift and the Lord of the Settled Account is also the Lord of the Reward.

Some aspects of what the master says are pretty much what we would expect: *Well done, good and faithful servant.* Imagine receiving this commendation from God! But there is a surprise here as well. The master doesn't say, *Now you can float on lovely fluffy clouds, and live in a very nice condo with lots of upgrades, and sing in the choir that will sing the same songs for a hundred billion years.*

Instead he says, "You have been trustworthy in *a few things.* Now I will put you in charge of *many things.*"

Now it is time for you to get on with your real work! Remember, the master had given the servant an enormous amount of wealth. Yet he says, "You have been trustworthy in *a few things.*" Can this be true—that greater wealth than any of them had seen or imagined amounts to *a few things?* From this story of the talents we learn that heaven will be nothing at all like an eternal retirement village. In fact, heaven will be that place where we finally experience the fullness of adventure, creativity, and fruitfulness we were made for.

So why don't you take a moment to ask some questions:

- What is my deepest dream?
- How much passion do I experience in my daily life?
- How often do I take risks that require a power greater than my own?

You can drift: get up, go to work, come home, eat supper, watch TV, retire, and die.

Or, you can take each moment and say, "God, this is yours."

You may have lavish talents—resources of finances or networks or abilities that could produce huge returns for the Lord of the Gift—and you're just sitting on them. It's time for you to get in the game. The Lord of the Gift can take five fish and two loaves and feed the multitudes. The Lord of the Gift can take twelve bumbling followers and create a community that has spread throughout the world with a dream that refuses to die.

He can take what you have to offer and make a difference that matters for eternity.

Peter answered him, "Lord, if it is you, command me
to come to you on the water." He said, "Come."
MATTHEW 14:28–29

DISCERNING
THE CALL

Living means being addressed.
MARTIN BUBER

A man appears before the pearly gates.
   "Have you ever done anything of particular merit?"
St. Peter asks.

"Well, I can think of one thing," the man offers. "Once
I came upon a gang of high-testosterone bikers who were
threatening a young woman. I directed them to leave her
alone, but they wouldn't listen. So I approached the largest and most heavily tattooed biker. I smacked him on the
head, kicked his bike over, ripped out his nose ring and
threw it on the ground, and told him, 'Leave her alone now
or you'll answer to me.'"

St. Peter was impressed. "When did this happen?"

"A couple of minutes ago."

There is a big difference between faith and foolishness.
Historically, commentators have differed on whether Peter's

desire to leave the boat was an expression of devotion or an impulse control problem. Calvin said it was given as a warning against "over-much rashness" and foolish risk taking. On the other hand, Chrysostom viewed this as an act of a disciple's love; he noted that Peter did not say in pride, "Bid me walk on the water," but in devotion, "Bid me come unto thee."

Whichever way you view it, one of the striking aspects of the story as Matthew tells it is that Peter does not immediately jump out of the boat. He begins by requesting Jesus to give him permission first. ("Lord, if it is you, command me to come to you on the water.")

Matthew's portrait of Peter makes it quite clear that he was in touch with his inner impulsive child. So why does he pause here to ask for a command first before climbing out of the boat?

I believe that Matthew wants his readers to understand a crucial aspect about water-walking: Peter is not in charge of water-walking—Jesus is. This is not some power at Peter's disposal to use anytime he chooses, for whatever purpose he pleases. Jesus is looking for something more than mere impulsiveness. Sometimes people make reckless decisions—about relationships, finances, or work—and then rationalize it with a veneer of spiritual language. So it is worth considering for a moment what water-walking is not.

Israeli scientists have identified what is being called the risk-taking gene. People identified as excitable and curious had a longer version of a gene known as D4DR than reflective and laid-back subjects. Type Ts engage in what have come to be known as "extreme sports": mountain climbing, parasailing, hang gliding, and BASE jumping. It is possible for us to make courageous, high-risk decisions that are stupid.

The line between "Thou shalt not be afraid" and "Thou shalt not be ridiculous" is often a fine one and not easily located. Knowing when to get out of the boat and take a risk does not only demand courage; it also demands the wisdom to ask the right questions, the discernment to recognize the voice of the Master, and the patience to wait for his command.

Jesus is not looking for impulse-ridden Type Ts. He is looking for what might be called the Type W, or water-walking personality. This involves the desire for adventure with God—the God-gene—and we all have one. It is part of our spiritual DNA. It requires both courage to take risks and wisdom to know which risks to take.

CALLING: A REFLECTION OF GOD'S IMAGE

We begin with a theological question: What does God do all day?

If you had to answer that question in a single word, what would you say? Think he mostly sits around watching stuff?

The biblical writers tell us what God does in a single phrase: He works.

Leland Ryken notes that Christianity is quite unique in this regard. The ancient Greeks, for instance, viewed the gods as being above work. Mount Olympus was a kind of divine Palm Springs where, aside from hurling the occasional thunderbolt, Zeus and his associates lived in Leisure World. In contrast, the opening lines of Genesis are filled with God's work—he separates light from darkness, makes the sky and heavenly bodies, gathers the waters, forms human beings from dust.

And after the sixth day, God does not go into retirement. The psalmist is quite clear that the universe does not run by mechanical necessity; it is run by God.

> You make springs gush forth in the valleys;...
> From your lofty abode you water the mountains;
> > the earth is satisfied with the fruit of your work.
> You cause the grass to grow for the cattle,
> > and plants for people to use....
> O Lord, how manifold are your works!

God is particularly active in working with people. The psalmist says that the God of Israel will "neither slumber nor sleep," but is always guiding and protecting his flock.

When Jesus came to earth, he came as a worker. In fact, for most of his adult life he worked as a carpenter. Jesus leaves no doubt that he works, for he says, "My Father is still working, and I also am working."

God is described in the Bible by many metaphors that involve work: He is a gardener, an artist, a potter, a shepherd, a king, a homemaker, and a builder.

"The God of the Bible," writes Paul Minear, "is preeminently a worker" : "The Lord God formed man from the dust of the ground, and breathed into his nostrils the breath of life; and the man became a living being."

You are a piece of work by God! If you have ever had someone, maybe a boss or a spouse, say sarcastically to you, *"You're a piece of work,"* it is literally true. And because you were made in God's image, you were also created to do work. You were made to create, lead, study, organize, heal, cultivate, or teach. I want to invite you to go for a walk.

The Bible is, among other things, a list of unforgettable walks. The first one was taken by God himself, who, we are told, used to walk in the garden in the cool of the day. But as a general rule, God asked people to walk with him.

There was the hard walk that Abraham took with his son Isaac on the road to Moriah. There was the liberating walk Moses and the Israelites took through the path that was normally occupied by the Red Sea, and the frustrating walk that took them on the roundabout way of the desert for forty years. There was Joshua's triumphant walk around Jericho, the disciples' illuminating walk to Emmaus, Paul's interrupted walk to Damascus.

But perhaps the most unforgettable walk of all was taken by Peter the day he got out of a boat and walked on the water. It is unforgettable not so much because of where he was walking as what he was walking *on* and who he was walking *with*. In this book, let Peter's walk stand as an invitation to everyone who, like him, wants to step out in faith, who wants to experience something more of the power and presence of God. There is a consistent pattern in Scripture of what happens in a life that God wants to use and improve:

- There is always a call.
- There is always fear.

- There is always reassurance. God promises his presence.
- There is always a decision. Sometimes, as with Moses and Gideon, people say yes to God's call. Sometimes, as with the ten frightened spies or the rich young ruler who spoke with Jesus, they say no.
- There is always a changed life. Those who say no are changed too. They become a little harder, a little more resistant to his calling, a little more likely to say no the next time.

I believe that this pattern from Scripture continues today. Gregg Levoy notes that in Scripture, God often calls to the prophets by repeating their names twice: "Abraham, Abraham. Jacob, Jacob. Moses, Moses." Once is not always enough.

So how do ordinary human beings go about discovering their callings?

TAKING YOUR CALLING SERIOUSLY

This is not how God works. He does not make spare parts. *You* are not a spare part. You have a purpose—a design that is central to God's dream for the human race. We are, first of all, according to Scripture, called to know God, to receive his love and mercy, and to be his children. We are called to live in the reality of his kingdom and to have Christ formed in us.

John Belushi and Dan Ackroyd once starred in a movie

called *The Blues Brothers*. They played a couple of ex-convict-wanna-be musicians who were trying to raise money for an orphanage. Anytime they were asked about their work, they had a standard response: "We're on a mission from God." They always said it as if they believed it. The very idea that two inept, unworthy human beings could be on a mission from God was the central joke of the whole story.

Here is the story of your life: You are on a mission from God.

Either that is true, or you have no purpose, no mission at all. Jesus put it like this: *You are the salt of the earth. You are the light of the world.* Others have come before you. Others will come after you. But this is your day. If God's kingdom is to manifest itself right now, it will have to be through you. God himself will not come to take your place. *You are on a mission from God.*

I can wear my calling lightly. I can live free of the fear of failure, without being preoccupied by how my career looks to others, knowing my salvation and worth as a person are not at stake in my job title.

But what we do matters immensely. It is worth devoting our best energy to. *We are on a mission from God.*

HONORING YOUR RAW MATERIAL

In addition to taking it seriously, discerning a calling requires one of the greatest challenges of self-exploration and judgment a human being can undertake. Callings are usually not easy to discover.

The whole idea of a calling is taken from Scripture, where time after time God calls someone to do his work. The whole idea of calling is that there is a Call-er and a call-ee.

Parker Palmer, a Quaker educator and writer, says this: "Everything in the universe has a nature, which means limits as well as potential." One of the competencies of artistry and craftsmanship is knowing how to discern the nature of the material you are working with. Great sculptors spend much time studying a piece of marble before they ever take a chisel to it. You also have a nature with your own potential and limits. Frederick Buechner wrote that calling is "the place where your deep gladness meets the world's deep need." It is not hard to figure out where the world's deep need is. It is everywhere! What turns out to be more difficult than you might expect is discovering where your deep gladness lies. What work brings you joy? For what do you have desire and passion—for these, too, are gifts from God. This is why giftedness is about more than just talents—it includes *passion*. As Arthur Miller says, "It's the lifeblood of a person, the song that her heart longs to sing, the race that his legs were born to run.... There's an electricity associated with giftedness. Give a person the chance, and he'll jolt you."

One of my favorite pictures of the "deep gladness" that God intends for his creation is in Psalm 19, where the psalmist says, "In the heavens he has set a tent for the sun, which comes out like a bridegroom from his wedding canopy, and like a strong man runs its course with joy." That strong man exults in the race, and runs it, with everything he's got. So too do the teacher, the business leader, the writer, the gardener, the accountant, the nurse, and the mechanic.

That does not mean that following a calling always brings feelings of enjoyment. Often it means the gritty resolution to bear with a hard task when it would be easier to quit. But even this yields a certain satisfaction when I know I have been skilled and fitted by God for the task. Parker Palmer's wonderful book *Let Your Life Speak* has much to say about discovering one's vocation. He writes about the time when, because of his growing prominence in educational circles, he was offered the presidency of an educational institution. It would have meant an increase in pay, status, and influence— from a career standpoint, it was a no-brainer.

But the Quakers have a tradition where, when faced with an important decision about calling, they gather a half-dozen friends to serve as a "clearness committee." This committee gathers primarily to ask questions so as to discern God's calling more clearly. For a while the questions were easy—what would Parker's vision be for this school; what mission would it serve in society, and so on. Then someone asked what appeared to be a very simple question: "Parker, what would you like about being president?"

Oddly enough, Parker had to think about this one for a while. "Well, I wouldn't like all the politics involved; I wouldn't like having to give up my study and teaching; I wouldn't like to have to raise funds...."

"Yes," the questioner reminded him, "but the question was what *would* you like?"

"I'm coming to that," he said irritably, then proceeded to list several more irksome things. "I wouldn't like to have to give up my summer vacations, I wouldn't like..." Finally Parker answered that he supposed he'd like getting his picture in the paper, with the word "president" underneath it.

If Palmer had taken the job, think of what the results would have been in his life: fatigue, discouragement, a loss of joy, lack of energy, and a sense of inadequacy. "You cannot choose your calling," Palmer says. "You must let your life speak." Perhaps you were created to learn and, by your learning, to benefit others. You will find yourself drawn to reading, reflecting, writing, and teaching. But if you are convinced that you must be a corporate success for your life to count, you will saw against the grain of your life. You will refuse to let your life speak.

Maybe you are a woman who loves to lead teams, to sound trumpets and charge up hills. But if you have been told that women are not to do such things, that you must stay in the background, you will bury the gift you were given. You will refuse to let your life speak.

It is very important to distinguish what I love doing for its own sake from what I may want to do because of the rewards it may bring me.

Sometimes this choice—the decision to let one's life speak—has spelled the difference between failure and greatness. William McFeely's biography of Ulysses Grant describes a man who was masterfully fitted for military but horribly ill-equipped for business and politics. In his final—and extraordinary—State of the Union message, he apologized for his ineptness: "It was my fortune, or misfortune, to be called to the office of Chief Executive without any previous political training."

Why, then, did this Civil War hero work so hard for

a job he neither enjoyed nor understood? "His personal need was to retain the immense respect in which he was held everywhere in the North.... He wanted to matter in a world he had been watching closely all his life. A little recognition—a little understanding that he did know what he was doing—was all he required. He did not truly love the job—it is as if he merely desired his picture in the paper with the word *president* under it.

When I do not honor my raw material, reality becomes my enemy. I close my eyes and ears to all the indications that I am trying to pursue what I am not called or gifted to do. But underneath I am condemned to live in chronic, low-grade anxiety that whispers to me that I am trying to be someone I'm not.

If I have the courage to acknowledge my limits and embrace them, I can experience enormous freedom. If I lack this courage, I will be imprisoned by them. Some of my limitations do not bother me much. It does not really concern me that I am unable to operate power tools or draw a straight line. But I have a few limitations that are exceedingly painful to me. I think of people I know who possess tremendous minds. They have a depth of learning and insight that enables them to make lasting contributions to the search for truth and knowledge. They sit at the table of what philosopher Mortimer Adler calls the "Great Conversation" of the human race. I was bright enough to do well in school and reach a certain level of learning, but I will never have a mind like that. I will not sit at the table.

Even as I write these words, I recall failures that are the most disappointing to me. Many years after they occur, the memory of my failures still holds the power to make me want to forget them, hide from them, or explain them away. The reason for some of these failures was not simply a lack of persistence or unfriendly circumstances (which might just call for more effort).

I think of the dreams I had for a church I helped plant that did not grow into what those of us at the core hoped and prayed it might become. I know that, as least in part, my limitations played a role. I am convinced that if I face up to acknowledging the limitations that pain me most, there is enormous freedom and joy on the other side.

I believe that each of us has similar experiences, which is why I think some of the most important, yet difficult questions for a person to ask are *What is your most painful limitation? What is the limitation that frightens you most to acknowledge and accept? Where do you most avoid seeing the deep truth about yourself?*

ASSEMBLE YOUR OWN "CLEARNESS COMMITTEE"

Likewise, one of the hardest commands in Scripture to obey is Paul's statement to regard yourself with "sober judgment." To come to an accurate assessment of my passions, gifts, and limits is one of the great challenges of life. In part, this command requires tremendous self-awareness. But I am also likely to need some help from other people to overcome my blind spots.

When I think of the value of receiving discernment

from more than one person, from a "clearness committee," I think of Bob Buford. Bob was an immensely successful television tycoon who sensed God was calling him to get out of a very well-appointed boat. In the words of his book *Halftime*, he wanted to move from "success to significance." He and his wife, Linda, met at length with one adviser, who helped him clarify his sense of purpose immensely. Then this adviser suggested a questionable next step: "Sell your company and invest in the ministry-oriented projects you've been talking about." Bob writes,

> I sat there, stunned by the implications of this decision. Linda appeared no less stunned. I could almost see the stereotypical images of ministers, missionaries, and monastics passing through her mind. Would we be a philanthropic couple passing out money until our sack was empty? Would we be required to dress like a minister and his spouse?

Bob goes on to explain how he assembled his own clearness committee (though he didn't use that language). Together they helped him see that what he loves most and does best involves strategic thinking and organizational leadership. They discerned that if he were to sell his company, he would lose a platform that could be leveraged for a great deal of good. Instead, they helped him see that his passions and competencies were ideally suited to help pastors and church leaders deal with issues of organizational complexity and mission effectiveness. Today he leads a ministry that develops leadership for key churches throughout the country—*and loves doing it*. But if he had run out and followed his first adviser's counsel—if he had sold his business and simply doled out the funds—he never would have experienced the effectiveness or fulfillment that he has today.

In the Quaker tradition, a clearness committee does not come together to give you advice. (Lots of people will do that without your asking.) And it certainly does not need people who have their own agenda for your life. The primary job of this group is simply to ask questions, listen thoughtfully, and then pray for a sense from God for his calling on your life.

CONDUCT "LOW-COST PROBES"

Since discerning a calling usually requires time and patience, and most of us have bills that must be paid—what do we do while we are searching? This process is bad news for those of us who want to microwave everything, including our vocations. We may be tempted to jump into commitments too rashly.

One alternative is to conduct what Bob Buford calls a "low-cost probe." The idea is to keep your day job, but test the waters of a new calling. Begin to explore your effectiveness in the area to which you believe God may be calling you. Further, Gordon Smith notes that discernment honors previous decisions and commitments. God is a careful worker and does not waste any resources.

Maybe for you a low-cost probe would involve a short-term mission plunge, or taking on a commitment to teach at your church, or getting involved as a volunteer launching a new ministry. Take confidence in the fact that there is biblical precedent for launching a low-cost probe. Amos transitioned into the prophecy business but still had his shepherding position to fall back on. Even Paul apparently kept his tent-making operation in production mode while he went into church planting.

A Calling Often Involves Pain

People sometimes romanticize the notion of vocation. Receiving a calling from God is not the same thing as falling into your dream career. A dream career generally promises wealth, power, status, security, and great benefits. A calling is often a different story.

God called Moses: *Go to Pharaoh—the most powerful man on earth. Tell him to let his labor force leave without compensation to worship a god he doesn't believe in. Then convince a timid, stiff-necked people to run away into the desert. That's your calling.*

And Moses said: *Here am I. Send Aaron.*

God called Jonah: *Go to Nineveh—the most corrupt and violent city in the world. Tell its inhabitants—who don't know you and won't acknowledge me—to repent or die.*

And Jonah said: *When's the next whale leaving in the opposite direction?*

God called Jeremiah to preach to people who wouldn't listen. It was so hard and Jeremiah cried so much that he became known as the Weeping Prophet.

As a rule, the people whom we read about in Scripture

who were called by God felt quite inadequate. When God called Abraham to leave home, or Gideon to lead an army, or Esther to defy the king, or Mary to give birth to the Messiah, their initial response was never: *Yes, I'm up to that challenge. I think I can handle that.*

The first response to a God-sized calling is generally fear.

This doesn't mean that God calls us in a way that violates our "raw material." Where God calls, God gifts.

It does mean, though, that natural talent alone is not enough to honor a calling from God. I will need ideas, strength, and creativity beyond my own resources to do what God asks of me. It will have to be God and me doing it together. We are not called just to work *for* God. We are called to work *with* God.

Everyone in Scripture who said yes to their calling had to pay a high price. So will you and I.

HAVING A CAREER VERSUS HAVING A CALLING

A calling, which is something I do *for* God, is replaced by a *career*, which threatens to *become* my god. A career is something I choose for myself; a calling is something I receive. A career is something I do for myself; a calling is something I do for God.

A career may end with retirement and lots of "toys." The significance of a calling lasts for eternity. A career can be disrupted by any number of events—but not a calling.

Scripture is full of people who were pressed into slavery, captured and sent into exile, thrown into prison. Their career trajectories did not look promising, but they fulfilled their callings in extraordinary ways.

Sometimes, in the providence of God, the end of a career is the beginning of a calling. And you have a calling. You are not a spare part—you are on a mission from God.

He said, "Come." So Peter got out of the boat, started
walking on the water, and came toward Jesus.
MATTHEW 14:29

WALKING ON
THE WATER

*I went to the woods because I wished to live
deliberately . . . and not, when I came to die, discover
that I had not lived.*
HENRY DAVID THOREAU

In some ways, the high point in the story of Peter
comes in the middle of the passage. It is contained
in a single phrase: *Peter . . . started walking on the water.*
There are many other parts to the story—the storm; the
fear that came before this and the fear that would follow;
the failure and critique. These are all important parts to
the story, and we learn from them because we are familiar with storms, fear, and failure. We may ignore or deny
them at our peril.

I think that during those moments Peter was storing up
memories he would carry to his grave: the feel of the water
somehow standing solid beneath his feet; the rush of the

wind in his face; the startled looks of the boatmen as he passed them by (a moment I'll bet he enjoyed immensely). I think he knew this was the walk of his life.

IT IS WORTH THE RISK

I love to read of how Jesus's confidence contrasted with his disciples' fear. Once, in a different boat, a tremendous storm was raging. Jesus was taking a nap even as the disciples were convinced they were going to die. When they woke him up, Jesus was not afraid at all. He just went to the side of the boat and addressed the wind: "Peace! Be still!"

Most people I know love to hear stories and images about the powerful God we serve. But there is the problem: That information alone is not sufficient enough to create courageous human beings.

Here is a powerful question I first heard many years ago to help me know whether I am getting out of the boat in any area of my life: What am I doing that I could not do apart from the power of God?

If you were to ask Peter that question, the answer would be very simple and straightforward. It was clear that the only way Peter would be able to stay afloat was if God took over. How about you? Is there any challenge in your life right now that is large enough that you have no hope of doing it apart from God's help? If not, consider the possibility that you are seriously underchallenged.

If you want to walk on the water, you have to be willing to get your feet wet first. When I take the risk of confessing a sin to another person, I discover that God really will honor truth-telling—but I have to get my feet wet first.

When I risk using my spiritual gift, I can know the joy of being used by God—but I have to get my feet wet first.

God promised Moses and the Israelites freedom. He did deliver them from Pharaoh, but first they had to act in trust. They had to march to the Red Sea *before* he parted it.

Over and over in Scripture this pattern is repeated:

Naaman has to wash seven times in the water *before* he is cured of leprosy. Gideon must winnow his army from 32,000 down to 300 *before* God will deliver them from the Midianites. The loaves and fishes must be relinquished *before* they can be multiplied. The seed must be buried in the earth and die *before* it can be raised to greater and more fruitful life.

If I am going to experience a greater measure of God's power in my life, it will usually involve the first-step principle. It will usually begin by my acting in faith—trusting God enough to take a step of obedience.

HOW FAITH GROWS

I believe an important reason why God so often asks us to take a first step has to do with the nature of faith and how it grows. Most people I know wish, at least at certain points in their lives, that they had more faith. I know of people who torment themselves over having too little of it.

When people wrestle with doubt, they may tell themselves that they will try harder to have more faith. But faith is not the sort of thing that can be acquired by trying harder. Imagine if someone were to say to you, "I find myself doubting Old Faithful. I'm just not sure it can be trusted." What would your advice be? Not "Try harder to believe!" The best advice for such a person would be, "Just hang around Old Faithful. Get to know Old Faithful better." And because Old Faithful is faithful, the better you know it, the more you will trust it.

It is the same with God. Never try to have more faith—just get to know God better. And because God is faithful, the better you know him, the more you will trust him.

How much faith do I need? Not a feeling of certainty. Just enough faith to take a step.

Expanding Your Spiritual Comfort Zone

Most of us have an area that might be called our "spiritual comfort zone," which is the area where we feel most comfortable trusting God. When God calls us to go beyond our spiritual comfort zone, we begin to feel nervous or uncomfortable.

For example, we might be comfortable talking about God with church friends, but nervous about explaining our faith to someone who does not believe. We might be comfortable in our current job, but anxious about the possibility that God wants to do some vocational realignment. We might feel enough faith to pray for people we are in relationship with, but confronting someone who has been behaving badly toward us would make us cringe. We might discuss past problems smoothly enough, but the idea of honestly naming our current struggles to a trusted friend would send us running.

There is only one way to increase your spiritual comfort zone, and acquiring more information alone will not do it. You will have to follow the Path of God, which requires taking a leap of faith.

Where is God calling you to walk on the water? Let me give you four indicators that may help you to know, and I will tell you about some real-life water-walkers along the way.

THE INDICATOR OF FEAR

Very often God will ask us to step out of the boat at the point of our fears—precisely because he wants us to overcome them. For instance, one of the most exciting spiritual adventures in life is helping another human being find God. What keeps us from getting out of the boat evangelistically? The number one reason is fear. Fear of what? Historically, people have risked their livelihoods and even their lives for their faith. In many parts of the world, Christians still do. But for most of us, the worst-case scenario is that the other person will not want to talk about spiritual matters. We may experience a brief sense of embarrassment or rejection. When we ask, "Would you like to talk about spirituality?" the other person may say, "No, I don't think so. Not today. Thanks anyway." That is about the most pain we face.

On the other hand, we might actually be part of God's redemptive purposes on earth.

Jeffrey Cotter tells about one time—an unforgettable

plane ride—when he took the risk. As a pastor returning from a job interview and dressed in blue jeans, he
found himself sitting next to a pinstripe-wearing, attaché
case-carrying, *Wall Street Journal*-reading businessman.
Cotter was struck by the man's pride in his work and
accomplishments. Cotter realized he had been in avoidance
mode during the whole flight because of fear.

Looking skeptically at Cotter's clothing, Mr. MBA
asked about his line of work. Let Cotter tell it from here:

"It's interesting that we have similar business inter-
ests," I said. "You are in the body-changing business;
I'm in the personality-changing business. We apply
basic theocratic principles to accomplish indigenous
personality modification."

"But do you have an office here in the city?"

"Oh, we have many offices. We have offices up
and down the state. In fact, we're national; we have at
least one office in every state of the union, including
Alaska and Hawaii. As a matter of fact, we've gone
international. And Management has a plan to put at
least one office in every country of the world by the
end of this business era."

"You mentioned management. How do they make
it work?"

"It's a family concern. There's a Father and a
Son . . . and they run everything."

"It must take a lot of capital," he asked, skeptically.
My friend sat back in his seat. "What about with
you?" he asked.

"The employees? They're something to see," I said. "They have a 'Spirit' that pervades the organization."

"But do you have good benefits?"

"They're substantial," I countered with a gleam. "I have complete life insurance, fire insurance—all the basics. You might not believe this, but it's true: I have holdings in a mansion that's being built for me right now for my retirement. Do you have that in your business?"

"You know, one thing bothers me. I've read journals, and if your business is all that you say it is, why haven't I heard about it before now?"

"That's a good question," I said. "After all, we have a 2,000 year old tradition.... Want to sign up?"

THE INDICATOR OF FRUSTRATION

Sometimes people in Scripture get motivated to trust God in remarkable ways when they grow frustrated with the brokenness of a fallen world.

David could not tolerate a pagan Philistine giant taunting the God of Israel. He was moved to risk his life in the name of his God.

Even in the world today, it is often at the point where we are frustrated by the gap between fallen reality and our sense of God's desires that we are moved to action in a cause greater than ourselves.

An outstanding example of this was a woman named Henrietta Mears. Miss Mears taught college-age, single young people for decades at Hollywood Presbyterian

Church. She was a formative influence on the life of a whole generation of Christian leaders including Billy Graham, Bill Bright, former Senate Chaplain Richard Halverson, and hundreds of others. She was frustrated at not being able to give her students first-rate material to educate them, so she began a little publishing enterprise out of a garage. It grew into Gospel Light Publishers, one of the most effective Christian publishers of its day.

At the end of her remarkable life, as she lay on her deathbed, someone asked her, "Miss Mears, if you had it all to do over again, would you do anything differently?"

She thought for a moment. "If I had it all to do over again—I would have trusted Christ more."

THE INDICATOR OF COMPASSION

Toby was the ring bearer at our wedding. He looked like a waif out of a Dickens novel—big china blue eyes, white-blond hair, skin the color of alabaster, named Toby. Not long after our wedding, Toby's family moved, and we lost touch. Years later, a new coworker turned out to be a good friend of Toby's family and told us what our ring bearer had been up to. When Toby was in high school, he wrote an essay on world hunger and ended up winning a two-and-a-half week study tour in Africa through World Vision.

Toby was not only struck by the beauty of Ethiopia, but also by the rampant poverty. One day during his trip, he was at a World Vision distribution camp, handing out food and supplies and playing with some of the local kids. As Toby and the other World Vision personnel were getting ready to leave, an eleven-year-old-boy tapped him on the shoulder. The boy stared at Toby's T-shirt. Then he looked down at his own shirt, which was thin, dirty, and filled with holes. He looked back at Toby and shyly asked, "Could I have your shirt?"

As they drove away, the weight of that one request gripped Toby and would not let him go. The memory of that scene haunted him the rest of the trip. Everywhere he went, Toby saw that boy's face. He organized a T-shirt drive called "Give the Shirt Off Your Back." He started collecting them door-to-door. He persuaded some 7–11 stores to set bins. The next thing Toby knew, he had collected over 10,000 T-shirts.

Then he was faced with another problem. How do you get two tons of T-shirts from Michigan to Ethiopia? He called one relief agency after another, telling them his story. He received always the same answer: "We'd like to help, but it's too expensive." Finally, Toby was put in touch with an outfit called Supporters of Sub-Sahara Africa. They happened to be taking a shipment of supplies to Africa and agreed to take his T-shirts along for the ride. There was just one hitch: They could take them to only one country. Would it be all right, they wanted to know, if the shirts went to Ethiopia?

THE INDICATOR OF PRAYER

One of my favorite adventures in prayer involves Doug Coe, who has a ministry in Washington, D.C. that mostly involves people in politics and statecraft. Doug became acquainted with Bob, an insurance salesman who was completely unconnected with any government circles. Bob became a Christian and began to meet with Doug to learn about his new faith.

One day, Bob came in all excited about a statement in the Bible where Jesus says, "Ask whatever you will in my name, and you shall receive it."

"Is that really true?" Bob demanded.

Doug explained, "Well, it's not a blank check. You have to take it in context of the teachings of the whole Scripture on prayer. But yes—it really is true. Jesus really does answer prayer."

"Great!" Bob said. "Then I gotta start praying for something. I think I'll pray for Africa."

"That's kind of a broad target. Why don't you narrow it down to one country?" Doug advised.

"All right. I'll pray for Kenya."

"Do you know anyone in Kenya?" Doug asked.

"No."

"Ever been to Kenya?"

"No." Bob just wanted to pray for Kenya.

So Doug made an unusual arrangement. He challenged Bob to pray every day for six months for Kenya. If Bob would do that and nothing extraordinary happened, Doug would pay him five hundred dollars. But if something remarkable did happen, Bob would pay Doug five hundred dollars. Bob began to pray, and for a long while nothing happened. Then one night he was at a dinner in Washington. The people around the table explained what they did for a living. One woman said she helped run an orphanage in Kenya—the largest of its kind.

"You're obviously very interested in my country," the

woman said to Bob, overwhelmed by his sudden barrage of questions. "You've been to Kenya before?"

"No."

"You know someone in Kenya?"

"No."

"Then how do you happen to be so curious?"

"Well, someone is kind of paying me five hundred dollars to pray...."

She asked Bob if he would like to come visit Kenya and tour the orphanage. Bob was so eager to go, he would have left that very night if he could.

When Bob arrived in Kenya, he was appalled by the poverty and the lack of basic health care. Upon returning to Washington, he couldn't get this place out of his mind. He began to write to large pharmaceutical companies, describing to them the vast need he had seen. He reminded them that every year they would throw away large amounts of medical supplies that went unsold. "Why not send them to this place in Kenya?" he asked.

This orphanage received more than a million dollars' worth of medical supplies.

The woman called Bob up and said, "Bob, this is amazing! We've had the most phenomenal gifts because of the letters you wrote. We would like to fly you back over and have a big party. Will you come?"

So Bob flew back to Kenya. While he was there, the president of Kenya came to the celebration, because it was the largest orphanage in the country, and offered to take Bob on a tour of Nairobi, the capital city. In the course of the tour they saw a prison. Bob asked about a group of prisoners there.

"They're political prisoners," he was told.

"That's a bad idea," Bob said brightly. "You should let them out."

Bob finished the tour and flew back home. Sometime later, Bob received a phone call from the State Department of the United States government:

"Is this Bob?"

"Yes."

"Were you recently in Kenya?"

"Yes."

"Did you make any statements to the president about political prisoners?"

"Yes."

"What did you say?"

"I told him he should let them out." And he did.

How about you? What are you praying for? Give it six months. I won't promise you five hundred dollars, but I will give you a refund on the cost of this book. To the contrary, if something extraordinary does happen, you have to write and tell me about it.

But when he noticed the strong wind, he became frightened, and beginning to sink, he cried out, "Lord, save me!" Jesus immediately reached out his hand and caught him, saying to him, "You of little faith, why did you doubt?" When they got into the boat, the wind ceased.

MATTHEW 14:30–32

SEEING THE WIND

Jesus promised those who would follow him only three things . . . that they would be absurdly happy, entirely fearless, and always in trouble.

GREGG LEVOY

U ndaunted Courage is Stephen Ambrose's best-selling account of the Lewis and Clark expedition. After two years of battling nearly insurmountable problems—hunger, fatigue, desertion, hostile enemies, severe illness, and death—the party had reached the headwaters of the Missouri River. All their advance information had led them to believe that once they reached the continental divide, they would face about a half-day portage, and then reach the waters of the Columbia River and float safely to the Pacific Ocean. The hard part was behind them. Or so they thought.

Meriwether Lewis left the rest of his party behind to climb the bluffs that would enable him to see the other side, hoping to see the waters that would carry them the rest of the way. Imagine what he felt when, rather than seeing a gentle sloping valley as expected, he laid his eyes on the Rocky Mountains!

What do you do when you think your biggest problems are behind you, only to find out you have just been warming up? How do you rally the rest of the troops? Eventually, crossing the Rocky Mountains would be perhaps the supreme achievement of the whole trip. This challenge would call forth enormous creativity and perseverance; it would lead them to spectacular sights and unforgettable memories; it would build tremendous confidence.

Peter was on his way to hero status. The hard part was behind him—getting out of the boat. He was mastering this water-walking business. Then it happened—reality set in. "He saw the wind."

The same thing happens to us.

We see the wind. We face obstacles. Unexpected conflict saps our spirit. Plans go awry. People we were counting on let us down. Just when we were hoping for easy portage and smooth sailing, we are looking at the Rocky Mountains. What happens next?

Here is where things get interesting. There is a field in the social sciences that explores what has come to be known as resiliency. Researchers study people who have survived traumatic ordeals—when life did not turn out the way they planned. Some of the classic cases involved 3,000 prisoners of war who returned from "brainwashing" experiences in

Korea, 550 men who lived through captivity in Vietnam, and 52 hostages released after fourteen months of imprisonment in Iran. Other studies include survivors of World War II concentration camps, victims of crippling accidents, and children from very difficult backgrounds.

These studies have found that people generally respond to traumatic problems in one of two ways. Many are simply defeated by such difficult conditions, as we might expect. But some are marked by *resiliency,* a condition whereby they enlarge their capacity to handle problems and, in the end, not only survive but grow. What makes the difference? How do you endure in the face of a storm? Why do the Rockies energize some people and defeat others?

The answers have centered on a few themes:

- Resilient people continually seek to reassert some command and control over their destiny rather than seeing themselves as passive victims.
- Resilient people have a larger than usual capacity for what might be called moral courage—for refusing to betray their values.
- Resilient people find purpose and meaning in their suffering.

These qualities are not just the product of a strong character. Each of them grows out of a deep dependence on God. So let's take a look at a storm facer and mountain climber in Scripture by the name of Joseph. First we will find out how he was introduced to the Rockies. Then we will see how three qualities gave him a remarkably resilient faith.

GOOD NEWS/BAD NEWS

Growing up, I always liked good news/bad news stories—where details keep turning the story from triumph to tragedy and back.

Joseph's life is about to become a good news/bad news story.

Joseph is his daddy's favorite: That's very good.

But his brothers hate his guts: That's very bad.

His daddy gives him a beautiful coat: That's very good.

But his brothers rip it off, cover it with blood, pretend he's dead, sell him into slavery in a distant land: That's very bad.

He lands a job in Egypt's Silicon Valley working for Potiphar—this is very good.

Potiphar's wife thinks he's good-looking and tries to seduce him. This is very bad.

Joseph resists. Very good.

But the wife is furious. She lies to her husband and gets Joseph arrested. Since Egypt does not have good sexual harassment legislation on the papyrus at this time, Joseph is shafted. Very bad.

In prison Joseph meets Pharaoh's butler, interprets a dream that predicts the butler will get paroled, and arranges for the butler to get Joseph's release. Very, very good.

But the butler forgets, and Joseph languishes in prison. Very, very bad.

We wonder: How will it end? What matters in any good news/bad news story is the last turn. How does it end? If it ends with bad news, all the good that went before it is just a cruel farce that raises false hopes. If it ends with good news, the entire story gets redeemed.

WEARING THE ROBE

Joseph wore the Robe. The Robe said he was the chosen one—the golden boy. It meant he never had to wonder if his father loved him. It was the promise of a charmed life.

In a hundred ways—ways that most parents are not even aware of, but kids see a mile away—Jacob's favoritism for Joseph leaked out of him. One day, though, it took a most concrete form: He gave Joseph the Robe.

The Hebrew word to describe this garment is uncertain—"a long coat with sleeves," some translations put it. The Greek translation of the Old Testament—the Septuagint—called it the "coat of many colors"; and that is what the King James Version says, and that is how it looks in most of our imaginations.

Joseph wears the Robe quite often—it makes him feel special. It feels like a promise, perhaps, that he will never be alone, that he will never be merely "normal," that he will always have his father's protection and will be spared the problems others face. But every time he wears it, it is a reminder to his brothers that they will never be loved by their father the way Joseph is loved. Every time he wears it, they die a little inside.

That beautiful robe becomes a death shroud for the family. One day his brothers decide they cannot endure it for another day, so they tear the Robe off Joseph and sell him into slavery. He is just in the foothills—the Rockies are still ahead. Joseph's problems are just beginning. Joseph is about to get a front-row look at the wind.

POWERFUL DREAMS

Joseph not only wore the Robe but also dreamed big dreams of his destiny.

Listen to my dream, Joseph tells them. There was a field of sheaves, when suddenly my sheaf rose and stood upright, and all your sheaves gathered around and bowed down to mine. This means one day I will rule over all of you. I will command; you will submit. You will bow down in humble expression of your obedience to my authority. Isn't that cool? Aren't you happy for me? Let's play "bow down sheaf" now to practice.

The writer makes their response very clear: "So they hated him even more because of his dreams and his words." Serious sheaf envy.

Then Joseph has another dream. You'd think that by now he has learned to keep his dreams to himself. But he is so captivated by his dreams that the thought apparently does not cross his mind.

FACING THE STORM

Then one day Joseph was attacked by his brothers, sold to a traveling caravan, carried off to a distant land, and purchased as a slave by a family he did not know.

Joseph saw the wind.

It is hard enough to get out of the boat when the wind is calm and the water's smooth. But in life that is rarely the case. Sooner or later the storm strikes—in your marriage, work, ministry, finances, or health. It is in the act of facing the storm that you discover what lies inside you and decide what lies before you.

What are the key decisions that facing the storm forces?

RESILIENT PEOPLE EXERCISE CONTROL RATHER THAN PASSIVELY RESIGN

POWs and hostages who triumph over adversity share a common trait—they managed to reassert a sense of command over their future. Instead of becoming passive, they focused as much attention as possible on whatever possibilities for control remained.

Through exercise regimens, games, messages sent to one another, POWs reminded themselves that their bodies had been captured but their spirits had not.

Far from home, separated from his father, betrayed by his brothers, kidnapped by slave-traders, surrounded by strangers—the writer says, "The Lord was with Joseph." Imagine what happened to his courage and confidence when he found out that after the worst had happened to him, it led to the best! The Lord was with Joseph. He could face the Rockies after all!

Even though it wasn't his dream, even though his dream seemed dead, Joseph applied himself diligently to the task at hand. I would have been tempted to give up.

There is a progression in the story. We are told that

Joseph was "in the house," meaning that he was not simply a worker in the field. He had been promoted to work in the house. He was management.

Then the text says, "Joseph found favor in his [Potiphar's] sight and attended him"—now he is executive assistant. After this, Potiphar names him overseer; Joseph becomes CEO of the whole operation. Potiphar's trust is so complete that he never even asks to look at the books. "So he left all that he had in Joseph's charge; and, with him there, he had no concern for anything but the food that he ate."

Because Joseph did not quit, he set in motion the development of his potential, the deepening of his faith and endurance. That faith would one day enable him to become the most effective leader in Egypt and fulfill the part God intended for him to play in the rescue of his family and the redemption of the world.

What if Joseph had lived in a spirit of passive resignation? He would have missed his destiny. Quitting is always easier than enduring. It is always easier to stop and have a donut than to run another lap, or to stomp out of a room in anger than to stay and seek to resolve the conflict.

When life does not turn out the way you had planned, the option of quitting will always begin to look like sweet relief:

- "This marriage is difficult, I just want out. Or, even if I don't seek an outright divorce, I'll just settle for mediocrity. I'll quit trying."
- "Seeking to live on a budget and honor God with a tithe is just too hard. I'm going to spend!"

Growth happens when you seek or exert control where you are able to rather than giving up in difficult circumstances. It happens when you decide to be wholly faithful in a situation that you do not like and cannot understand. It happens when you keep walking even though you see the wind. Then you discover that, somehow, you are not alone. As he was with Joseph, the Lord is also with you.

But then Joseph runs into trouble of another kind. Potiphar's wife "cast her eyes on Joseph" and said to him, "Lie with me." This is not a subtle approach. It brings us to another crossroad.

RESILIENT PEOPLE REMAIN COMMITTED TO THEIR VALUES WHEN TEMPTED TO COMPROMISE

Now Joseph must wrestle with temptation. Joseph could have thought, *Where is God? I'm far from home, hated by my brothers, isolated from my father. I wore the Robe, but now I'm a slave, and a slave is all I'll ever be. I'll never have what my father has, what I dreamed of having, what I deserve to have—my own life, wife, family, property, and name. Why shouldn't I reach for what little happiness I can get? It's not like I have anything to lose.*

But Joseph says no.

He speaks of the trust that Potiphar has placed in him and about the significance of honoring trust. His life and world are given meaning by loyalty and honoring relational commitment. To follow another way would be to enter a world of darkness that would destroy life as he knows it.

Potiphar's wife persists: "And although she spoke to

Joseph day after day, he would not consent to lie beside her or to be with her." The implication of that last phrase is that she may have moderated her demand in hopes of getting Joseph to take the first step—just a small step over the line. "Let's just be together for a while." Still Joseph refuses.

Finally she decides to force the issue:

> One day, however, when he went into the house to do his work, and while no one else was in the house, she caught hold of his garment, saying, "Lie with me!" But he left his garment in her hand, and fled and ran outside.

There are times, when life does not turn out the way you planned and temptation has a very strong hold on your garment, when the only thing to do is run.

A friend of mine, an executive, told me about a business trip that did not go well. An account that he thought he had sewn up went horribly wrong. Sitting in a hotel lounge, lamenting his failure, lonely and bored, he was unexpectedly approached by "Potiphar's wife." A temptation that he would normally not have given a second glance suddenly felt irresistible.

My friend knew the temptation of Joseph, the temptation that comes when life does not turn out the way he planned. If Joseph had given in here, he would have betrayed the one who trusted him, would have betrayed God, and would probably never have known his destiny. Instead, he ran. We know what he ran away from—from Potiphar's wife, from Ms. Temptation beckoning him to the blue light. We are told that he ran outside, but I wonder if when he got outside he found himself running to God. I wonder if he did not pour out his heart—all the disappointment and aloneness that made temptation so painful. But don't think it is ever enough just to run away from sin. Sin is a pretty dogged pursuer. Sooner or later, you have to turn and face the pain that makes the temptation so attractive. Sooner or later, you have to run to God.

Mrs. Potiphar stands there with his garment in her hand. Once more Joseph will be stripped of his robe and have it used against him. She calls to the household, "See, my husband has brought among us a Hebrew to insult us. He came in to lie with me, and I cried out in a loud voice; and when he heard me raise my voice and cry out, he left his garment beside me and fled outside."

Potiphar must see through this floozy. Joseph must be rewarded.

Nope. Potiphar goes on the warpath, Joseph goes to prison, and Mrs. Potiphar goes home, presumably to wait for a more compliant slave.

We are not to the end of the story yet. There's more bad news. But in the middle of the bad news comes a familiar phrase: "The Lord was with Joseph and showed him steadfast love; he gave him favor in the sight of the chief jailer."

Resilient People Find Meaning and Purpose in the Storm

Warsaw psychiatrist Adam Szymusik found that survivors who had taken no strong convictions into the Nazi death camps with them did not fare as well over time as those who felt they suffered for their political or religious views. Studies of suicide notes have found that they rarely mention problems like failing health, rejection, or financial crises. Rather, they speak of being "tired of life" with suicide as "a way out." As psychologist Julius Segal puts it, "Countless individuals beset by trauma report that their basic problem is an existence that is without meaning." We know that Joseph, even in prison, was filled with meaning and purpose: "But the Lord was with Joseph...." To use the language of theophany and the words "pass by"—a moment when God appeared on earth to select an individual to communicate a message, as to Moses, Elijah, Jesus—the Lord wanted to pass by Joseph—in prison!

And so the Lord came to Joseph just as he came to the disciples, in a storm.

> But the Lord was with Joseph and showed him steadfast love; he gave him favor in the sight of the chief jailer. The chief jailer committed to Joseph's care all the prisoners who were in the prison, and whatever was done there, he was the one who did it.

In prison Joseph initially found meaning in a very simple way—by helping a couple of cell mates, a baker and a butler. One morning, after they had troubling dreams, we're told, "When Joseph came to them in the morning, he *saw* that they were troubled. So he asked Pharaoh's officers, who were with him under house arrest, 'Why are your faces downcast today?'"

FINDING COMPASSION
IN THE STORMS

This is a striking detail in the story. It would be easy for Joseph to become isolated, to focus only on his own disappointment. When life does not turn out the way you plan, you forget that other people face disappointment too. You may begin to think only about your own hurts. Your world becomes so small that your pain is the only pain you notice. This is the death of the heart, the loss of meaning.

Instead, Joseph realizes that he is not the only one for whom life has not turned out according to plan. He lives the way Jesus would. He treats disgraced prisoners like human beings—he notices them, asks about them, and expresses genuine interest in them.

At a time when we would expect him to be self-preoccupied, Joseph is sincerely concerned for others' well-being: "Why are your faces downcast today?" he says to his fellow prisoners, a butler and a baker. He does this even though he is not expecting anything in return. And by his noticing, Joseph gives meaning to his presence in prison. And someone notices them. Someone cares about their lives. Words can do this. Every positive word you speak boosts someone's hope a bit.

I wonder if part of the meaning of Joseph's suffering was to develop his compassion.

In the midst of the storm, do you read the faces of people around you the way Joseph did? Most people wear on their faces what is going on inside of them.

Do you look at your friends, coworkers, people who serve you, or children in your life, and *notice* if their faces are downcast?

STORMS TEACH WHAT NOTHING ELSE CAN

It may have been no accident that Joseph spent years as a slave and then as a prisoner in jail before he was ready to be exalted to a prominent position and be used by God. Storms have a way of teaching what nothing else can.

Now, in prison, he *noticed*. His suffering gave him eyes of compassion.

The prisoners explain to Joseph that each of them has had a troubling dream. Joseph takes a moment to offer help: "Do not interpretations belong to God? Please tell them to me." The butler tells of his dream about a vine and grapes. Joseph replies, "Within three days Pharaoh will lift up your head and restore you to your office."

The baker is greatly encouraged by this and shares his dream about birds and cakes. Joseph replies, "Within three days Pharaoh will lift up your head—*from you!*—and hang you on a pole."

And the baker says, "That's the last time I tell you one of my dreams."

The butler is released. This is good news. Joseph has arranged for the butler to speak a good word in his behalf, to get him released.

Imagine Joseph's joy! He will be set free. No more

prison. No more slavery. He can return to his father. He can go home.

He waits through the first day. Nothing. *Maybe tomorrow*, he says to himself. *Tomorrow will be celebration day.*

The next day passes. Again, nothing. He tells himself it is just some red tape. He thinks perhaps the butler is just waiting to make sure his timing is right.

Days turn into weeks, then months, and still Joseph sits, rotting in prison.

Eventually it becomes clear: The butler forgot. He has his own life. People tend to be obsessed with their own well-being. For two years, nearly as long as it took Lewis and Clark to cross a continent, Joseph sat alone. I wonder how often he thought this might be the end of his story.

God was not finished yet. Joseph would learn to see the deeper meaning of his suffering. As he would put it to his brothers, "Even though you intended to do harm to me, God intended it for good, in order to preserve a numerous people, as he is doing today."

Dallas Willard writes,

I meet many faithful Christians who, in spite of their faith, are deeply disappointed in how their lives have turned out. Often, due to circumstances or wrongful decisions and actions by others, what they had hoped to accomplish in life they did not. They painfully puzzle over what they may have done wrong, or whether God has really been with them.

All of Joseph's best days—his rise in Egypt, his service

to a nation, his impact as a leader, his reunion with his father, his reconciliation with his brothers—all lay on the other side of the Rockies. And that is because ultimately his story was a part of God's story.

Much of the distress for people comes from a failure to realize that their lives lie before them. What is of significance is the kind of people they have become. God eventually sent one more dreamer, he ended up being another young man for whom things did not seem to turn out the way he had planned. Crowds mocked him, friends abandoned him, Peter denied him, Judas betrayed him, soldiers crucified him, and his body was laid in a tomb—one more dreamer, one more young man whose life turned out to be a disappointment.

Until . . . on the third day . . . he woke up feeling good. Ultimate resiliency.

On the third day, bad news lost for all time.

Ever since that third day, whatever bad news may enter your life has no power to separate you from God.

But when the disciples saw him walking on the sea, they were terrified, saying, "It is a ghost!" And they cried out in fear. But immediately Jesus spoke to them and said, "Take heart, it is I; do not be afraid."

Peter answered him, "Lord, if it is you, command me to come to you on the water." He said, "Come." So Peter got out of the boat, started walking on the water, and came toward Jesus. But when he noticed the strong wind, he became frightened, and beginning to sink, he cried out, "Lord, save me!"
MATTHEW 14:26–30

CRYING OUT IN FEAR

Nothing is so much to be feared as fear.
HENRY DAVID THOREAU

The single command in Scripture that occurs more often than any other—God's most frequently repeated instruction—is formulated in two words:

Fear not.

So why does God tell human beings to stop being afraid more often than he tells them anything else?

I think God says "fear not" so often because fear is the

number one reason human beings are tempted to avoid doing what God asks them to do.

A PARABLE OF COURAGE

A two-year-old girl stands by the side of a pool. "Jump!" her father says, with open arms. "Don't be afraid. You can trust me. I won't let you fall. Jump!"

She is, in that moment, a bundle of inner conflict. On the one hand, everything inside her is screaming to stay put. The water is deep, cold, and dangerous. She has never done this before. She can't swim. On the other hand, that is her daddy in the water. He is bigger and stronger than she is and has been relatively trustworthy up to this point for the past two years. He seems to be quite confident about the outcome.

The battle is between fear and trust.

Trust says, *Jump!*

Fear says, *No!*

If she chooses to jump, she will become a little more confident of her father's ability to catch her. She will become more likely to take the leap next time. The water will hold less terror for her. Ultimately, she will come to see herself as the kind of person who will not be held back by fear.

On the other hand, if she decides not to jump, that will also have consequences. She will lose the opportunity to discover that her father can be trusted. She will be a little more inclined toward safety next time. She will perceive herself as the kind of person who does not respond bravely to challenges. She will work harder to make sure she avoids being faced with decisions involving fear in the future.

There is a place for fear. But I want trust to be stronger. I never want the *no* of fear to trump the *yes* of faith.

Fear makes two appearances in the story of Jesus walking on the water. First, the disciples are afraid because they do not understand that Jesus is with them in the storm. Dale Bruner writes,

So Jesus says, "Courage! I AM! Fear not!" As we saw in chapter 1, Jesus is not just identifying himself ('It's me'); this is a revelation that the God "I AM" is in their midst.

A young disciple stood in the boat. Jesus stood on the water. Jesus stretched out his hands and said, "Come."

Trust said, *Jump.*

Fear said, *No.*

Peter jumped. And for a while, everything went smoothly.

Then fear struck a second time. He saw the wind. And this led to the next phase—he became frightened. His response to the wind and the storm was to give in to fear. He lost his sense of confidence that Jesus was master of the situation. He did not just sink in the water, but sank in his own anxiety and worry.

I believe the reason God says "fear not" so often is that fear will sink us faster than anything else.

A young man finds himself engaged to a woman with whom he is not in love—but everyone is expecting the marriage to take place. Fear keeps him from being aware of what truly lies within his heart and acting with authenticity.

An elderly man is afraid of dying. He has never told

anyone this—he is afraid of what others might think of him if they should find out.

I have enormous admiration for people who genuinely struggle with fear, but in the moment of decision choose to jump. It is one thing when a Type T jumps. But for someone to whom risk does not come naturally to stand in the boat and jump when God calls; for someone who wrestles with worry and doubt and yet still obeys, trembling but trusting—*that is true courage.*

WHAT IS FEAR?

At its simplest and most benign, fear is an internal warning cry that danger is nearby and we had better do something about it. It is designed to be what researchers call a "self-correcting mechanism"—to be unpleasant enough to motivate us to take action and remove ourselves from whatever is threatening us. It readies our body to flee, hide, or fight.

There is a large physiological component to fear. A friend of mine was once trying to prepare for an upcoming conversation with a very intimidating person. He was talking about this with his wife and told her, "You know, when I think about doing this, my palms get sweaty."

About an hour later, unable to think of anything else, he said, "You know, when I think about doing this, my mouth gets dry."

Her advice to him: "Why don't you just lick your palms?"

Fear involves several things. First, your mind senses you are in danger. Certain experiences like loud noises or seeing extreme heights seem to be hard-wired into us to produce fear from birth. Scientists speak of some fears as innate while others are learned.

The incredible speed of this process helps us react immediately to potential trouble, but it also means our initial responses have not been filtered yet by a slower process—what has been called the rational fear system. This is why, for instance, people on roller coasters or in horror movies can be simultaneously terrified and laughing—the primitive fear system is screaming that we are in danger while the rational fear system tells us we are okay.

There is such a thing as good fear: the fear that keeps a child from touching a hot stove, the fear that keeps you from driving recklessly, the fear that keeps a man from dressing the way he really wants to—in bold plaid colors that express his true personality—because he is afraid of what his wife may say.

If fear only happened when it was truly needed—when you are about to be struck by a truck or chased by a homicidal maniac—it would be nothing to worry about. The problem is that for most of us, fear strikes when it is neither helpful nor wanted. It can get attached to what does not truly threaten us and can become paralyzing instead of motivating.

In some cases fear ceases to be sporadic and becomes habitual. When this happens, we become *worriers*. Worry is a special form of fear. The traditional distinction is that fear is caused by an *external* source while worry or anxiety is produced from the *inside*. Yet they produce the same physical responses. Worry is fear that has unpacked its bags and signed a long-term lease.

We need to take the physical aspect of fear seriously. It is a natural part of being human. An article in the *New York Times Magazine* cited research that indicates some people have a strong predisposition toward fear and anxiety that is apparently genetic.

For the most part, the number of commands in the Bible suggests that fear generally plays a destructive role in the lives of men and women. Fear, as you and I usually experience and handle it, is not a good thing.

Over and over in the Bible, it is *fear* that threatens to keep people from trusting and obeying God.

To live in chronic fear extracts the highest cost of all. Susan Jeffers puts it like this: "Pushing through the fear is less frightening than living with the underlying fear that comes from a feeling of helplessness." So let's consider the high cost of living in a mindset of fear.

LOSS OF SELF-ESTEEM

All research suggests that self-esteem largely boils down to one issue: When you face a difficult situation, do you approach it, take action, and face it head on, or do you avoid it, wimp out, and run and hide?

If you take action, you get a surge of delight, even if things do not turn out perfectly. *I did a hard thing. I took on a challenge.* You grow.

When you avoid facing up to a threatening situation, even if things end up turning out all right, inside you say, *But the truth is, I wimped out. I didn't do the hard thing. I took the easy way out.*

Avoidance kills an inner sense of confidence and esteem.

This is why praise from others, even when it is sincere, often does not help much. Avoiders become experts at "impression management"—pretending to be what they think will be acceptable to others. But when you take on a challenge, it builds the core of who you are, even if you don't perform flawlessly.

Why don't you conduct your own experiment of trust this week? Sometime when you are tempted to avoid, hold your ground and press forward instead:

Stand up to a bully who is mistreating others (or you) at work. Wade feet first into a task that you have been putting off because you have feared it would be difficult or unpleasant. Acknowledge to God in prayer a sin or character flaw you have been trying to hide.

When you do this, you will get a little stronger inside.

But when you wimp out by refusing to take the difficult step or saying the hard word—you die a little. And if that becomes a pattern, over time you come to see yourself as someone who cannot cope with life's greatest challenges.

LOSS OF DESTINY

I had lunch recently with a friend who is clearly being called by God to do some tremendous things in life. He is an enormously gifted person—a talented artist and a terrific writer. Yet he is in a job that is killing him. It doesn't call on his greatest abilities, and he has no passion for it. He is just punching the time clock. Why does he stay in it?

Fear. More specifically, the fear of failure. In an odd way, he is also afraid of success. If he succeeds, people may expect more from him. Eventually, if this pattern does not change, it will come time for my friend to retire, and he will be relieved to quit and will try to be as comfortable as he can for the remaining years of his life.

And he will never have done what God created him to do, never have become what God created him to be. Fear will cost him his destiny—and that is too high a price to pay.

LOSS OF JOY

Have you ever met a deeply joyful, chronically worried person? Fear destroys joy. Live in it, and you will know the pain of constant, chronic, low-grade anxiety. Transcend it, and you will know delight.

Another friend of mine is up to his neck in a very difficult challenge. The stakes—relationally, emotionally, and spiritually—are extremely high. "I have never been so far out on a limb with God," he told me. "I keep telling the other people involved, 'Trust him! God really will work!' And now all I can think is—*he better!*" I looked at my friend and saw in his face all the marks of someone courageously seeking to trust and obey—excitement, anticipation, suspense, prayer, a deep sense of dependence, significant activity, being stretched to the capacity of his abilities. I realized that he is having the time of his life. On the other hand, giving in to fear is a joy-killer. According to current research, most worriers tend to have high-capacity imaginations. They usually carry above-average IQs. They are often people with much creative potential.

But their imaginations run toward the negative. They tend to catastrophize:

- What if bad things happen?
- What if I get in an accident and wreck the car?
- What if I lose my wallet?
- What if I preach a poor sermon?

All these things are contingent, set in the future, and may never happen at all!

LOSS OF AUTHENTIC INTIMACY

Fear and hiding go together like adolescence and hormones. The very first recorded instance of fear reflects this: *Where were you, Adam?*

I heard you in the garden, And I was afraid, because I was naked, so I hid.

And we have been hiding ever since—behind smiles we don't really feel, behind agreeable words we don't really believe, mostly behind the things we truly feel and believe but refuse to say.

When I was growing up, my parents would sometimes have my brother, sister, and me play "the quiet game." I imagine you know the rules: Whoever could be the quietest the longest wins. It is a popular game with parents.

I hate to say it, but sometimes—for altogether different reasons these days—I still play the quiet game. All too often I hold back from saying what I truly think or feel because of fear. I am afraid of what someone might think of me; or I am afraid of the pain in the conflict that might emerge; or I am afraid that I will have to spend more energy cleaning up the relational mess that will emerge than I really want to spend.

I wonder whom you might be playing the quiet game with: a boss? a spouse? an assertive relative? a strong-willed child? an opinionated coworker? an intimidating authority figure?

LOSS OF AVAILABILITY TO GOD

Fear whispers to us that God is not really big enough to take care of us. When I was seeing clients as an intern in graduate school, one of my clients had a phobia related to flying. She had gone through a traumatic experience on a plane as a little girl and had never quite recovered from it.

I had her go through a process called systematic desensitization, which involves learning to relax (it is physically impossible for the body to experience fear in a relaxed state) while having increasingly vivid mental pictures about flying, until eventually the person is able to fly. "Don't you know," I told her, "that God's with you everywhere? Some of Jesus's last words were, 'I am with you always.'"

There is no limit to his presence. There is no place where we can go, no activity we can engage in, where he is not watching over us.

I think of a woman who was in a dating relationship with a man although she knew it was not right. There were serious, unresolved sinful patterns in his life. She knew what was at stake. But if she broke up—she might be alone. She didn't think she could handle that, so she married him. And she is more alone now than she was when she was single.

What kept her in a relationship she *knew* she should break free of?

Fear.

She was afraid that God would not be adequate to protect her from unbearable loneliness.

And now she is headed for a mountain of regret. She wonders, "What if I had trusted him?"

What might have been? If I had trusted God—what might I have done? What might I have become?

It is a price too high to pay.

FEAR GETS PASSED FROM GENERATION TO GENERATION

Social science researchers say we are the most worried culture that has ever lived.

Life expectancy has more than doubled in the past century. We are able to cure more diseases than ever before. No group of human beings has ever been healthier, yet no group has ever been more worried about their health.

Journalist Bob Garfield tracked health articles in the *Washington Post, USA Today,* and the *New York Times* and discovered that, according to experts,

- 59 million Americans have heart disease
- 53 million suffer migraines
- 25 million have osteoporosis
- 16 million struggle with obesity
- 3 million have cancer
- 12 million have severe disorders such as brain injuries....

The results are that 543 million Americans are seriously sick—which is shocking in a country of 266 million people. As Garfield notes, "Either as a society we are doomed, or someone is seriously double-dipping."

The media frighten us because fear sells.

Government agencies are often set up so their continued funding depends on a public perception that they are protecting us from frightening risks.

Parents may have the worst time of all with fear. As parents your hopes, dreams, and callings are impaired by distorted fears and worry. Thus, you will be limiting the hopes, dreams, and callings of your children. They will learn from you that the only way to go through life is with anxiety and fear.

On the other hand, fear isn't the only thing that spreads. So does trust. Daring faith is contagious as well.

Sometime ago I took my then ten-year-old son parasailing. The man driving the boat said he could ascend to 400, 600, or 800 feet. "How high above the water do you want to fly?"

Johnny decided "I'm gonna go 800 feet up. I might be scared when I go up there at first. But I'm going to do it because the ride only lasts a few minutes. But once it's over, I'll have it forever."

I think if God had anything to say to you now, it might be this:

The ride only lasts a few minutes.

In the vast eternal scheme of things, your life is briefer than you could possibly imagine.

But whatever you do in faith,

every time you trust me,

that you will have forever.

Go ahead and jump.

So Peter got out of the boat, started walking on the water, and came toward Jesus. But when he noticed the strong wind, he became frightened, and beginning to sink, he cried out, "Lord, save me!" Jesus immediately reached out his hand and caught him, saying to him, "You of little faith, why did you doubt?"
MATTHEW 14:29–31

THAT SINKING FEELING

He who has never failed somewhere, that man cannot be great. Failure is the test of greatness.
HERMAN MELVILLE

When we are young, failure does not seem to affect us much. No one-year-old stumbles when he tries to walk, then says to himself, *Well, that was stupid and clumsy of me! I guess I wasn't cut out to be a walker. I sure don't want anybody else to watch me fall. I'd rather settle for crawling the rest of my life than put myself through that experience again.*

Children are perfectly content to put up with unsteadiness and falling on the way to walking. That is why we call them toddlers. It is all they are capable of doing. They *expect* to toddle.

But as we grow older, we seem to grow more afraid of falling. We would rather avoid going down than learn to walk.

Peter was a water-toddler. His steps, like his faith, were uncertain. He was willing to risk failure for the adventure of trusting Christ more fully. And Jesus is not about to treat Peter's failure as grounds for dismissal.

I believe this is one of the most important questions in life: *Why is it that for some people failure is energizing, while for others failure is paralyzing?*

People's perceptions of and responses to failure make an enormous difference in their lives—more than IQ, physical attractiveness, charm, and financial assets put together. Those who can learn from it, retaining a deep sense of their own value and marshaling the motivation to try again, become masters of failure management. The Old Testament Scriptures relate that for a long time David experienced a glittering string of successes. He was anointed by Samuel to be king of Israel. As a boy he defeated Israel's most formidable enemy—Goliath. King Saul chose him as a warrior and musician. The army loved him, the people wrote songs about him: "Saul has killed his thousands, David his ten thousands."

David knew what it was to walk on water. He trusted God, and for a long time everything he touched turned to gold. He was on his way to the palace.

Then a strange thing happened. One by one all those wonderful things he had been given were stripped away. David lost his job. He had been promoted from shepherd to court musician to warrior—the most successful officer in the army. But now Saul was jealous. He started chucking spears, and David was out of a job. With it, David lost his income and his security. He would never serve in Saul's army again.

Next, he lost his wife. He had married Saul's daughter, Michal, but Saul sent soldiers to kill David. Michal helped him escape, but she was taken back by Saul and ended up marrying someone else. David later got her back, as we read in 2 Samuel 3.

So David fled to Ramah, where Samuel, his spiritual mentor, lived. Samuel was the one who anointed David when he was young. Samuel was the one who assured David of God's presence in his life. But Saul heard where David went and sent soldiers after him. David had to make another escape, and Samuel could not go with him—he was an old man. Next, David ran to his best friend, Jonathan, who had stood up to his father, Saul, and risked his life for David. But Jonathan would not leave the court. He could not—or would not—raise the sword against his own father. So once more David was on his own and had to run for his life.

His job and marriage had ended in failure, his mentor had died, his best friend was out of his life. Then it got worse.

David fled his home and ran to Gath, hometown of the late giant Goliath. David had nowhere to go but to the Philistines, his mortal enemies. This move did not turn out to be any more successful than the others. David was

very much afraid of King Achish of Gath. So he changed his behavior before them; he pretended to be mad when in their presence. Achish said to his servants, " Look, you see the man is mad; why then have you brought him to me? Shall this fellow come into my house?"

Having failed to find a refuge in Gath, David ran once more. "David left [Gath] and escaped to the cave of Adullam."

THE CAVE NAMED FAILURE

Whereas once David had wealth, power, fame, friends, security, and what he thought was a guaranteed future, now he was running for his life and living in a cave.

It is called the cave of Adullam, but we might think of it as the cave named Failure. The cave is where you end up when your props, supports, and crutches get stripped away. Perhaps you are in the cave right now—

Maybe it is because you have lost your job, or you are under financial pressure. Maybe it is because your dreams about family life have been shattered. Maybe you have lost a mentor or a best friend; there was a relationship you counted on, and now it is gone. Maybe it involves a physical condition—you have lost your health. Or you may simply find yourself alone.

If you are not in the cave right now, wait a while—you will be. Nobody plans on ending up in the cave, but sooner or later everybody logs some time there.

The hardest thing about being in the cave is that you begin to wonder whether God has lost track of you. Did he forget his promises? Does he remember where I am?

There is one other thing you need to know.

Sometimes the cave is where you meet God, for God does some of his best work in caves.

David knew about failure. He spent about ten years of his life in the wilderness on the run. From a human perspective it looked as if God's promises to him would never come true.

He was not entirely alone. He did have some people come to him to form a little community. But they were not a very promising group. "Everyone who was in distress, and everyone who was in debt, and everyone who was discontented gathered to him; and he became captain over them." This was not the cream of the crop he had to work with; rather, they were bankrupt, agitated whiners. He and this motley crew established a kind of refugee community in a village called Ziklag. They had taken wives and started families, and periodically they would go raiding other villages.

One day they came home and discovered that their village was gone. Ziklag had been sacked, their wives and children carried off.

That sounds bad enough, but for David things could still get worse. His men's grief turned to anger—and their anger was turned toward David.

Then comes one of the great statements in Scripture: "But David strengthened himself in the Lord his God."

This is a great secret of spiritual life. When every other resource was gone, when every prop was kicked out from under him and every crutch taken away, when he reached the point of utter failure, David encouraged himself in the Lord.

How does this happen? I believe that the starting point in dealing with failure is to honestly face and name our discouragement. This is where David starts. We read about this in Psalm 142. This is a psalm for cave dwellers.

> With my voice I cry to the Lord;
>> with my voice I make supplication to the Lord.
> I pour out my complaint before him;
>> I tell my trouble before him.

Are you able to complain? If you can complain, you can take this step. Old Testament scholars tell us there are different kinds of psalms. But the single most popular and frequent category is called the psalm of lament, which consists of somebody complaining to God.

And God is apparently not put off by this at all. This is what David does in the cave. He gets quiet enough before the Lord to get to the bottom of his pain and discouragement. He feels it in his gut.

I have visited the churchyard where Shakespeare is buried in Stratford-upon-Avon. His body was put eighteen feet underground instead of the usual six to make sure no one would dig it up again. I have come to realize that I sometimes do that with my own sense of failure. I run for a class office at school, and lose. It tears at my need to have an image of a popular class leader; I feel low-grade embarrassment; I wish I had not run at all. But I don't talk about this with people. I do not even spend the time or effort to look deeply at it myself, to ask why it hurts, or what I might learn. I just want to put it eighteen feet under.

What I regret most as I look back is not that I failed. Rather, I regret feeling the pain of failure so keenly that

I backed away from owning it and learning from it, so I could not heal and move on. One day a man named Elijah found himself in a cave. He had been by any definition an extremely successful prophet, taking on four hundred opponents and an evil king and offering faultless weather forecasts to boot. But the opposition of a single queen triggered something in him. He was certain he had been a failure: "It is enough; now, O Lord, take away my life, for I am no better than my ancestors."

But God did not take away his life. God was very tender—he had an angel bake him a cake on hot stones and direct Elijah to get some sleep. All in all, God treated Elijah the way you do a cranky toddler—have a snack, take a nap, and we'll talk when you're a little more composed.

After a great wind, an earthquake, and fire came "a sound of sheer silence." And then came a still small voice, as God asked Elijah a wonderful question: "What are you doing here?" The best part of the question is that God did not say, "What are you doing *there?*" God was with Elijah in the cave.

But I think perhaps that the cave is the most wonderful place of all to find that you are loved by God. If you know—really know—that you are loved by God when you feel the weight of failure, then there is no place where you will be beyond the confines of his care.

It was in the cave that David cried out to God, "You are my refuge, my portion in the land of the living." When I know in the marrow of my bones that I am just as valued and loved by God when I have fallen flat on my face, then I am gripped by a love stronger than success *or* failure.

You can risk being fully honest with God for a very

important reason: God is never a God of discouragement. When you have a discouraging spirit or train of thought in your mind, you can be sure it is not from God. He sometimes brings pain to his children—conviction over sin, or repentance over fallenness, or challenges that scare us, or visions of his holiness that overwhelm us. But God never brings discouragement. Always, his guidance leads to motivation and life.

Some time ago I asked a spiritual mentor of mine, "How do you assess the well-being of your soul? How do you gauge your spiritual condition?"

My friend said that the first question he asks himself is this: *Am I growing more easily discouraged these days?* "Because," he told me, "if I'm walking closely with God, if I have the sense of God being with me, I find that problems lose their ability to damage my spirit."

TAKE ACTION

David's next step was to ask the priest to bring him the ephod—a sacred vestment worn originally by the high priest while ministering in the sanctuary—so he can inquire of the Lord what to do next. The ephod was a reminder of the presence of God.

David received a very clear message from the ephod: "Pursue; for you shall surely overtake and shall surely rescue." So he took action, and in doing so, he rescued his community and reclaimed his leadership.

Taking action is very powerful. The reason many people become paralyzed in discouragement is because they fail to devote the time or energy to understand what was involved in the failure in the first place, and then they fail to take action toward change. They wait for some outside force or person to rescue them when God is calling them to action.

In any arena where you are concerned about failure, the single most destructive thing you can do is *nothing*. Psychologist David Burns writes about what he calls the cycle of lethargy: When I'm faced with a challenge and I do nothing, it leads to distorted thoughts—that I am helpless, hopeless, and beyond change. These in turn lead to destructive emotions—loss of energy and motivation, damaged self-esteem, feeling overwhelmed. The end result is self-defeating behavior—procrastination, avoidance, and escapism. These behaviors then reinforce negative thoughts, and the whole cycle spirals downward.

The good news is that God has made us in such a way that taking one single step of action can be extremely powerful in robbing failure of its power. For example, take marital failure. Psychologist Neil Warren says that lack of hope is what kills marriage more than anything else. When hope dies, the motivation to change dies, and you quit trying. At that point, the death of the marriage is just a matter of time.

The alternative to taking action is passivity and resignation. One of Winnie the Pooh's friends is a gloomy donkey named Eeyore, who adopts this approach to life. Ward off the pain of discouragement by renouncing hope. This course must have been tempting to David at some points.

But you can know that is not God's will for your life. God is *never* a God of discouragement! Failure can be a tremendous motivator.

Parker Palmer writes about a time in his life when he experienced the cave of deep depression. His action step was to experience a program called Outward Bound.

I chose the weeklong course at Hurricane Island, off the coast of Maine. I should have known from that name what was in store for me; next time I will sign up at Happy Gardens or Pleasant Valley....

In the middle of the week I faced the challenge I feared most. One of our instructors backed me up to the edge of a cliff 110 feet above solid ground. He tied a very thin rope to my waist—a rope that looked ill-kept to me and seemed to be starting to unravel—and told me to start rappelling down that cliff.

After several unsuccessful attempts of hugging the cliff, and sliding helplessly down, my instructor said,

"The only way to do this is to lean back as far as you can. You have to get your body at right angles to the cliff so that your weight will be on your feet. It's counterintuitive, but it's the only way it works.

"You still don't have it," the instructor said helpfully, after a couple of more failed attempts.

"OK," I said, "tell me again what I am supposed to do."

"Lean way back," he said, "and take the next step." The next step was a very big one, but I took it—and, wonder of wonders, it worked. I leaned back into empty space, my eyes fixed on the heavens in prayer, made tiny, tiny moves with my feet, and started descending down the rock face, gaining confidence with every step.

I was about halfway down when I saw that I was approaching a deep hole in the face of the rock.

To get down, I would have to get around that hole, which meant I could not maintain the straight line of descent I had started to get comfortable with.

The second instructor let me hang there, trembling, in silence, for what seemed like a very long time. Finally, she shouted up these helpful words: "Parker, is anything wrong?"

In a high, squeaky voice, I said, "I don't want to talk about it."

"Then," said the second instructor, "it's time that you learned the motto of Outward Bound."

Then she shouted ten words that I hope never to forget, words whose impact and meaning I can still feel: "If you can't get out of it, get into it!"

This is your life. You can't get out of it. So get into it. Take one step toward trusting God in an area where you feel failure:

- Make a phone call to confront a situation that you've been avoiding.
- Open a book to begin studying for a project you have been putting off because it feels overwhelming.
- Write one letter to begin pursuing a job that would be a dream to you.

One small step of action is often worth a hundred internal pep talks. But you must remember one thing: You must be willing to fail.

In the movie *Chariots of Fire*, English runner Harold Abrams runs against the Scottish champion Eric Liddell and loses for the first time in his life. The pain of failure is so great he decides he cannot race again.

His girlfriend, Cybil, says, "Harold, this is absolutely ridiculous. It's a race you've lost, not a relative. Nobody's dead."

Harold moans, "I've lost."

"I know. I was there. I remember watching you; it was marvelous. *You* were marvelous. He was more marvelous, that's all. On that day the best man won.... He was ahead, there was nothing you could have done. He won fair and square."

"Well, that's that," Abrams says.

"If you can't take a beating, perhaps it's for the best."

"I don't run to take beatings—I run to win!" Harold shouts. "If I can't win, I won't run."

Cybil pauses, and then says to him firmly, *"If you don't run, you can't win."*

FAILURE AS TEACHER

Parker Palmer's story indicates another important part of failure management—taking the time and having the courage to learn from failure.

A book called *Art and Fear* shows how indispensably failure is tied to learning. A ceramics teacher divided his class into two groups. One group would be graded solely on quantity of work—fifty pounds of pottery would be an "A," forty would be a "B," and so on. The B group would be graded on quality. Students in that group had to produce only one pot—but it had better be good.

Amazingly, all the highest quality pots were turned out by the quantity group. It seems that while the quantity group kept churning out pots, they were continually learning from their disasters and growing as artists. The quality group sat around theorizing about perfection and worrying about it—but they never got any better. Peter was in the quantity group. His water-walking was not a piece of perfection. But after it was done, Jesus helped him learn about his failure ("You of little faith, why did you doubt?"). His faith wasn't "A" material yet. But it was at least a little stronger than that of the eleven disciples sitting in the quality group. Next time out, Peter's faith would be a little stronger.

The cave is the place where we can learn from failure and follow God's plans. One day Saul brought three thousand soldiers with him to search for David, and they rested just inside a cave, the same cave where David and his men were hiding. Saul and his soldiers were easy targets.

It must have been so tempting for David to think, *I could get out of the cave now. No more hiding. No more failure. I could be king.*

But he would not do it. In the cave David discovered that, more than he wanted to be king, he wanted to belong to God. He would rather please God and live in a cave than displease God and sit on the throne.

In the long run, being king—achieving outward

success—was not a big enough dream for David. He had a better dream—to please God.

Contrast what David learned with Willy Loman. Willy Loman is the central character in Arthur Miller's *Death of a Salesman*, one of the greatest plays about failure and broken dreams ever written. Willy has spent his life chasing the dream of being an irresistibly successful salesman. He tortures himself with the belief that if he were just persistent enough or self-confident enough, he would be a success, and that success would be the fulfillment of his dreams.

If he had had the courage to fully face the pain of his sense of failure, Willy might have perceived that he was pursuing the wrong dream and trying to be someone he was not. In the end, he commits suicide.

The cave of failure offers a precious chance to learn. But we must be willing to ask courageous questions:

- Am I chasing the right dream?
- Is what I'm pursuing consistent with God's calling on my life?

FINDING ULTIMATE REFUGE

In the cave David says to God, "You are my refuge." Of course, we know the rest of the story. We know that David will not die in the cave. We know there is a crown ahead.

Sometimes you are in a cave, and no human action can get you out. There is something you can't fix, can't heal, or can't escape, and all you can do is trust God. The Son of

David also lost his position, his status as a teacher, his safety and security. He lost not only his best friend, but all his friends, in spite of his teachings and warnings. But his failure got worse. He went to a cross and died. All his dreams, and all the dreams he inspired, appeared to die with him. And then they put his body in a cave. That was their big mistake. His body was there for three days. But they could not keep him there. They forgot that God does some of his best work in caves.

Jesus immediately reached out his hand and caught him, saying to him, "You of little faith, why did you doubt?"
MATTHEW 14:31

FOCUSING ON JESUS

Each of us carries a word in his heart, a "no" or a "yes."
MARTIN SELIGMAN

For in him every one of God's promises is a "Yes."
2 CORINTHIANS 1:20

The first time I ever skied was in the Swiss Alps. A friend who ran a winter sports camp flew my wife and me from Scotland, where we were living on the meager funds of a graduate fellowship, paid for our ski rentals, and bought us lift tickets. After two trips down the bunny slope, I told my wife, an avid skier, that I was ready for something more adventurous. We got on a chair lift, and it quickly rose hundreds of feet off the ground.

"Don't look down," I suggested.

We got off the chair lift and took something called a T-bar up the final ascent. Unfortunately, when we were almost to the top of the mountain, we fell off the T-bar. For a while we lay in the snow, waiting for the St. Bernard who never came. Dozens of skiers whizzed up the Alp beside us, yelling advice to us in German. The only word I could make out was "Dumköpf."

Another couple fell off (or jumped out of pity) at the same point. Hans could speak a little English, and he guided us in an hour through hip-deep snow to the nearest slope. The slope was marked by a black diamond with skull and crossbones. It went downhill at an angle of about eighty-five degrees.

Hans then gave me the only skiing lesson I have ever had. "Don't look down," he said. "You will be frightened by the slope and overwhelmed by the distance. When new skiers look down, they panic; and when they face straight ahead on a slope this steep—" He made a whistling sound and a motion with his hand that was not encouraging.

I suspect I pulled off the ugliest ski run that particular Alp had ever seen. Even when making snowplow turns, I would arrange whenever possible to execute them in front of small children so they could break my fall if necessary.

I got only one thing right: I never looked down. I became the world's expert at not looking down. It wasn't pretty, but it got me to the bottom of the hill.

When Peter was walking on the water, the text does not tell us whether Jesus said anything to him or not. But if he did, I imagine it being along these lines: *Peter, whatever you do—don't look down.* Peter did walk on the water. Then we are told three things happened. The focus of his attention shifted from Jesus to the storm—he saw the wind. This shift in attention gave rise to a new set of thoughts and feelings that focused on panic and inadequacy: "He became frightened." This in turn disrupted his ability to continue walking in Jesus's power—he began to sink and cried out, "Lord, save me!"

When Jesus rescued him, he asked Peter why he doubted. I do not think this was simply an exercise in blaming. I think that, like any good teacher, Jesus really did want Peter to learn from this experience so he could grow.

HOPE IS THE FUEL

While Peter's mind was focused on Jesus, he was empowered to walk on the water. But when his focus was on the storm, his fear short-circuited his ability to receive God's sustaining power.

There is a condition of the mind that is essential for us to live the kind of lives we are longing for. Call it hope, trust, or confidence. It is the single greatest difference between those who try and those who give up. When it is lost, like Peter, we are sunk. *Don't look down.*

Hope is the fuel that the human heart runs on. A car crash or a diving accident can paralyze a body, but the death of hope paralyzes the spirit.

Hope is why there are hospitals and universities.

Hope is why there are therapists and consultants and why the Texas Rangers keep going to spring training.

No composer would agonize over a score without the hope that some glimmer of beauty will emerge from the struggle.

Pablo Casals continued to practice the cello five hours a

day even though he was recognized as the world's greatest cellist, even when he had grown ancient enough that the effort exhausted him. Someone asked him what made him do it. "I think I'm getting better." That is hope.

Lewis Smedes writes that when Michelangelo was laboring day after day painting the ceiling of the Sistine Chapel, he grew so discouraged that he resolved to quit.

As the dusk darkened the always-shadowed Sistine Chapel, Michelangelo, weary, sore, and doubtful, climbed down the ladder from his scaffolding where he'd been lying on his back since dawn painting the chapel ceiling. After eating a lonely dinner, he wrote a sonnet to his aching body. The last line [was] . . . *I'm no painter.*

But when the sun shone again, Michelangelo got up from his bed, climbed up his scaffold, and labored another day on his magnificent vision of the Creator.

What pushed him up the ladder? Hope.

The story of every character God uses in the Bible is the story of hope.

Hope is what made Abraham leave his home.

Hope is what made Moses willing to take on Pharaoh.

We can survive the loss of an extraordinary number of things, but no one can outlive hope. When we forget this simple truth, we are like a steelworker walking on an I-beam three hundred feet in the air who begins looking down. When we become more focused on the overwhelming nature of the storm than the overwhelming presence of

God, we are in trouble. The Bible speaks of this often in terms of "losing heart."

Jesus never calls people to sink. It will surely happen sometimes—but it is not his intent; his call is never a set-up for failure.

Moses sent out twelve scouts to explore the Promised Land, to look at their enemies—people who defied God. Ten said they're too big. Two said, Let's go get them. All twelve looked at same land, faced the same situation, and reached two diametrically opposed conclusions.

Jesus and the disciples were in a boat when a storm came up. The disciples were so frightened, they were convinced they were going to die; crying out in panic, they lost heart. Jesus sat in the same boat, rode out the same storm—and took a nap.

In these stories, two sets of people faced exactly the same situation. They scouted the same Promised Land, endured the same storm. Some responded with peace, some with panic. Some lost heart, and some took heart.

Don't look down.

LEARNED HELPLESSNESS

What is the common denominator in the ten fearful spies and the Israelite soldiers who were paralyzed by Goliath?

One of the most influential psychology experiments of the twentieth century involved precisely this issue. Martin Seligman was a graduate student at the University of Pennsylvania in the 1960s when he stumbled onto an interesting phenomenon called "learned helplessness." It happened when some dogs were given slight electric shocks over which they had no control—no matter what the dogs did, they could not stop the shocks. The shocks simply stopped at random.

Later the dogs were placed in a situation where they could *easily* stop the shocks. They were put in a box that had a low barrier in the middle of it; all they had to do was step over the barrier to the other side and the shocks would stop. Ordinarily dogs learn to do this very quickly. When they are shocked, they start jumping around and discover that crossing the barrier brings relief. However, these previously shocked dogs had apparently learned something different—they "learned" that they were powerless to stop the shocks. They came to believe that no matter how hard they tried, nothing they did would make a difference.

Seligman describes the phenomenon this way: *"Learned helplessness* is the giving up reaction, the quitting response that follows from the belief that *whatever you do doesn't matter."*

Hope makes an extraordinary difference. Academic performance of freshmen at the University of Pennsylvania were predicted more accurately by tests that measured their level of optimism than by their SAT scores or high school grades. Daniel Goleman writes, "From the perspective of emotional intelligence, having hope means that one will not give in to overwhelming anxiety, a defeatist attitude, or depression in the face of difficult challenges or setbacks. Indeed, people who are hopeful evidence less depression than others as they maneuver through life in pursuit of their goals, are less anxious in general, and have fewer emotional distresses."

CHRIST-MASTERY

When someone comes to believe in God, to believe that he really is interested and active in human affairs, the issue of learned helplessness changes radically. Alburt Bandura is a Stanford psychologist who talks about "self-efficacy"—the belief that I have mastery over events in my life and can handle whatever comes my way.

But for one who believes in God, the hinge point is not simply what *I'm* capable of. The real question is what might God want to do through me. "I can do all things through Christ who gives me strength." Now, this is not a blank check. It means I have great confidence that I can face whatever life throws at me, that I never need to give up, that my efforts have potency—because of the One at work within me.

Here we see that optimism and hope are not quite the same thing. Optimism requires what Christopher Lasch calls a belief in progress. Hope includes all the psychological advantages of optimism, but it is rooted in something deeper. When I hope, I believe that God is at work to redeem all things *regardless of how things happen to be turning out for me today.* So let's think a while about what it means to cultivate a *mind* that is dominated by this one thought: "I can do all things through Christ who gives me strength." How do we go about developing minds that focus on Christ in the middle of storms?

What is your mind focused on?

Imagine getting the greatest performance car in the world and deciding you are going to take a serious run at the Indy 500 and dedicate yourself to winning it. What are the odds you would fill the tank with unleaded, low-octane gasoline from a thrifty-discount service station?

We are very aware that the fuel that goes into things ultimately determines their performance and well-being. What we feed everything else we possess is nothing compared with the importance of what we feed our minds. The apostle Paul wrote, "Whatever is true, whatever is honorable, or whatever is just, whatever is pure, whatever is pleasing, ... think about these things"—or in other words, "feed your minds."

Our ability to live in hope—to remain focused on Christ during the storm—is largely dependent on what we feed our minds. This is how we are able to focus on the Savior rather than the storm.

I want to introduce you to two laws that govern your life. The first is what might be called the *law of cognition:* You are what you think. Psychologist Archibald Hart writes, "Research has shown that one's thought life influences every aspect of one's being." Whether we are filled with confidence or fear depends on the kind of thoughts that habitually occupy our minds.

Over the last thirty years or so, the most dominant movement in American psychology is what is known as cognitive psychology—built around the truth that the way you think is the single most determinative thing about you.

The way you think creates your attitudes; the way you think shapes your emotions; the way you think governs your behavior; the way you think deeply influences your immune system and vulnerability to illness. Everything about you flows out of the way you think.

Paul said, "Do not be conformed to this world, but be transformed by the renewing of your minds."

The second law might be called the *law of exposure:* Your mind will think most about what it is most exposed to. What repeatedly enters your mind occupies your mind, eventually shapes your mind, and will ultimately express itself in what you do and who you become. The law of exposure is as inviolable as the law of gravity.

Children are exposed to thousands of acts of violence and murder on television and in even more graphic forms in movies. They see it on video games and observe symbols and images associated with gang violence glorified in pop culture—then we act surprised when a fight breaks out in the bleachers at a football game, or when shootings at Columbine High School or Sandy Hook devastate an entire nation. The truth is, we simply lack the national will and self-restraint to create a society that will produce minds that are not saturated with violence from the cradle on.

We are flooded with sexual images on television screens, computer terminals, magazine covers, and multiplex movie marquees. Sexually explicit images and emails are sent not just to teenagers, but to children who have virtually no chance to protect themselves from what they do not even know they are getting into—and then we profess to be shocked when promiscuity and sexual addiction levels go up and marital fidelity and stability go down.

It is amazing to me how often people think or live as if they could get away with violating the law of exposure. People will say, "I can read this material, watch these images, or listen to these twisted words—but it doesn't really affect me. I'm not really paying attention. It goes in one ear and out the other." Social scientists are coming to realize what writers of Scripture knew all along: Oh no, it doesn't!

Isaiah says, "Thou wilt keep him in perfect peace, whose mind is stayed on thee." It all depends on where your mind stays. The good news is that you can put these laws to work *for* you. If you really want to become a certain kind of person—a hopeful person focused on Christ—you must begin to think thoughts that will produce those characteristics.

UNDISCOVERED CONTINENTS OF SPIRITUAL LIVING

Frank Laubach devoted his whole life to learning to focus on Jesus. He was a sociologist, educator, and missionary to the Philippines in the early twentieth century whose career fell apart when he was in his forties. He lost the vocational opportunity he most desired. His plans for the Maranao people of the Philippines were utterly rejected. He and his wife lost three children to malaria, so she took their remaining child and moved a thousand miles away, leaving him desperately lonely.

In deep despair Laubach took his dog Tip and went to the top of Signal Hill, which overlooks Lake Lanao. He wrote,

> Tip had his nose up under my arm and was trying to lick the tears off my cheeks. My lips began to move and it seemed to me that God was speaking.

"My child . . . you have failed because you do not really love these Maranaos. You feel superior to them because you are white. If you forget you are an American and think only how I love them, they will respond."

I answered back to the sunset, "God, drive me out of myself and come and take possession of me and think thy thoughts in my mind."

This was the beginning of one of the remarkable spiritual experiments of the twentieth century. Laubach devoted the rest of his life to seeking to live each moment in conscious awareness of God's presence and carrying on a rich friendship with him.

Here are some thoughts based on his recommendations for staying focused on Christ:

- In a social setting, whisper "God" or "Jesus" quietly as you glance at each person near you.
- At mealtime, have an extra chair at the table to remind you of the presence of Christ.
- While reading a book or magazine—read it to him!
- When problem-solving at work, instead of talking to yourself about the problem, develop a new habit of talking to Christ.
- Keep a picture of Christ or a cross or a word from Scripture someplace where you will see it just as you're going to sleep.

The power of such practices, Laubach discovered, is not simply that they changed the patterns of his mind, though that in itself has considerable power. The real significance of this way of life is that it opened him wide to spiritual reality and power that was in fact all around him all the time.

Laubach went on to accomplish much worldwide in the areas of literacy and teaching, and he even counseled presidents. But the art he really mastered was focusing on Christ.

MEDITATION ON SCRIPTURE

Scripture talks about meditating on God's Word. The psalmist says that godly persons meditate on the Word "day and night." How much is that?

Do you know how to worry? If you can worry, you can meditate. To meditate merely means to think about something over and over. Memorizing Scripture is an important part of keeping a mind focused on Christ. This is a scary thought for many people. Maybe you find memorizing hard work. You have a hard time finding your car at mall parking lots; it takes you two or three attempts to get your child's name right (and you only have one child).

The point of memorizing Scripture is not to see how many verses you can memorize. The point is what happens to your mind in the process of rehearsing Scripture.

A friend recently sent me a card that read, "May the God of hope fill you with all joy and peace as you trust in him, so that you may overflow with hope by the power of the Holy Spirit."

When I think about that single statement, I am reminded that

- God is the source of all hope;
- He is even now seeking to fill my body with not just joy and peace, but *all* joy and peace;
- His desire is that I should not just contain hope, but *overflow* with hope;
- This process is dependent not on my power, but the power of the Holy Spirit at work in me.

KEEP YOUR FORK

One of the most important tools for focusing our minds involves rituals. I grew up in a tradition that was suspicious about the use of "ritual" in spiritual life, but in fact, rituals are generally indispensable for healthy human living.

A recent book for "corporate athletes" found that those who performed at the highest level used, among other things, a series of rituals that helped focus their minds and energies and enabled them to be fully present to their work.

So I have appropriated certain rituals and symbols that help keep my mind focused on Christ and hope:

- I have a nail in my office, about the size of the nails that might have been used on the cross. Sometimes in prayer I will hold it to remind me of what Jesus suffered for me.
- I have a statue of a little child, whose arms are

wrapped around a loving father. I look at that when I
pray, and I think of God loving me like that.

- I have a stone with a single word on it. It was given
  to me by a very good friend, who said that this is
  a quality that he sees in my life. Sometimes I pray
  about this word.

- I have a great prayer, framed for me and placed
  on the wall. It is attributed to St. Patrick many
  centuries ago. It is called "Lorica"—named for
  a Roman coat of armor that is meant for the
  protection of the one wearing it.

> *I arise today through God's strength to pilot me:*
> *God's might to uphold me,*
> *God's wisdom to guide me,*
> *God's eye to look before me,*
> *God's ear to hear me,*
> *God's word to speak for me,*
> *God's hand to guard me.*
> *Christ with me, Christ before me, Christ behind me,*
> *Christ in me, Christ beneath me, Christ above me,*
> *Christ on my right, Christ on my left,*
> *Christ when I lie down, Christ when I sit down,*
> *Christ when I arise.*
> *Christ in the heart of every one who thinks of me,*
> *Christ in the mouth of every one who speaks of me,*
> *Christ in every eye that sees me,*
> *Christ in every ear that hears me.*
> *I arise today*
> *Through a mighty strength, the invocation of the*
> *Trinity.*

What does a mind that is focused on hope look like? I read recently about a woman who had been diagnosed with cancer and was given three months to live. Her doctor told her to make preparations to die, so she contacted her pastor and told him how she wanted things arranged for her funeral service—which songs she wanted to have sung, what Scriptures should be read, what words should be spoken—and that she wanted to be buried with her favorite Bible.

But before he left, she called out to him, *"One more thing."*

"What?"

"This is important. I want to be buried with a fork in my right hand." The pastor did not know what to say. No one had ever made such a request before. So she explained. "In all my years going to church functions, whenever food was involved, my favorite part was when whoever was cleaning dishes of the main course would lean over and say, *You can keep your fork.*

"It was my favorite part because I knew that it meant something great was coming. It wasn't Jell-O. It was something with substance—cake or pie. So I just want people to see me there in my casket with a fork in my hand, and I want them to wonder, *What's with the fork?* Then I want you to tell them, *Something better is coming. Keep your fork."*

The pastor hugged the woman good-bye. And soon after, she died.

At the funeral service people saw the dress she had chosen, saw the Bible she loved, and heard the songs she loved, but they all asked the same question: "What's with the fork?"

So this week why not make the humble fork your own personal icon? When you pause to give thanks for the food, give thanks for your hope as well. Each time you wrap your fingers around the handle of a fork, remember: "Something better is coming."

When they got into the boat, the wind ceased.   9

MATTHEW 14:32

LEARNING TO WAIT

Waiting is the hardest work of hope.
LEWIS SMEDES

Waiting patiently is not a strong suit in American society.

A woman's car stalls in traffic. She looks in vain under the hood to identify the cause, while the driver behind her leans relentlessly on his horn. Finally she has had enough. She walks back to his car and offers sweetly, "I don't know what the matter is with my car. But if you want to go look under the hood, I'll be glad to stay here and honk for you."

We are not a patient people. We tend to be in a horn-honking, microwaving, Fed-Ex mailing, fast-food eating, express-lane shopping hurry. People don't like to wait in traffic, on the phone, in the store, or at the post office.

So how well do you wait?

At a tollbooth, the driver of the car in front of you is having an extended conversation with the tollbooth operator. You—

a. Are happy they are experiencing the tollbooth in

community. You think about joining them and
forming a small group.
b. Dream of things you would like to say to the
tollbooth operator.
c. Attempt to drive your vehicle between the other
guy's car and the tollbooth.

Most of us do not like waiting very much, so we like
the fact that Matthew shows Jesus to be the Lord of urgent
action. Three times in just a few sentences Matthew uses the
word *immediately*—always of Jesus: Jesus made the disciples
get into a boat and go on ahead of him "immediately." When
the disciples thought they were seeing a ghost and cried out
in fear, Jesus answered them "immediately." When Peter
began to sink and cried out for help, Jesus "immediately"
reached out his hand and caught him. Jesus's actions were
swift. Yet this is a story about waiting.

It was not until the whole episode was over that the
disciples got what they wanted—"the wind died down."
Why couldn't Jesus have made the wind die down "immediately"—as soon as he saw the disciples' fear? It would
have made Peter's walk easier. But apparently Jesus felt they
would gain something by waiting.

So, in this next-to-last chapter, before you rush out to
walk on the water, I want you to consider the activity that
Peter and the other disciples had to engage in right up to
the very end: waiting.

Let's say you decide to get out of the boat. You trust God.
You take a step of faith—you courageously choose to leave a
comfortable job to devote yourself to God's calling; you will

use a gift you believe God has given you even though you are scared to death; you will take relational risks even though you hate rejection; you will go back to school even though people tell you it makes no sense financially; you decide to trust God and get out of the boat. What happens next?

Well, maybe you will experience a tremendous, nonstop rush of excitement. Maybe there will be an immediate confirmation of your decision—circumstances will click, every risk will pay off, your efforts will be crowned with success, your spiritual life will thrive, your faith will double, and your friends will marvel.

Maybe. But not always. For good reasons, God does not always move at our frantic pace. Some forms of waiting—on expressways and in doctor's offices—are fairly trivial in the overall scheme of things. But there are more serious and difficult kinds of waiting:

- The waiting of a single person who hopes God might have marriage in store but is beginning to despair
- The waiting of a childless couple who desperately want to start a family
- The waiting of Nelson Mandela as he sits in a prison cell for twenty-seven years and wonders if he will ever be free or if his country will ever know justice
- The waiting of someone who longs to have work that is meaningful and significant and yet cannot seem to find it
- The waiting of a deeply depressed person for a morning when she will wake up wanting to live

- The waiting of a child who feels awkward and clumsy and longs for the day when he gets picked first on the playground
- The waiting of persons of color for the day when everyone's children will be judged "not by the color of their skin but by the content of their character"
- The waiting of an elderly senior citizen in a nursing home—alone, seriously ill, just waiting to die

Every one of us, at some junctures of our lives, will have to learn to wait.

Lewis Smedes writes,

Waiting is our destiny as creatures who cannot by themselves bring about what they hope for.

We wait in the darkness for a flame we cannot light,

We wait in fear for a happy ending we cannot write.

We wait for a not yet that feels like a not ever.

Waiting is the hardest work of hope.

Waiting may be the hardest single thing we are called to do. So it is frustrating when we turn to the Bible and find that God himself, who is all-powerful and all-wise, keeps saying to his people, *Wait*. "Be still before the Lord, and wait patiently for him.... Wait for the Lord, and keep to his way, and he will exalt you to inherit the land."

In the Bible, waiting is so closely associated with faith that sometimes the two words are used interchangeably.

The great promise of the Old Testament was that a Messiah would come. But Israel had to wait—generation after generation, century after century.

But even the arrival of Jesus did not mean that the waiting was over. Jesus lived, taught, was crucified, was resurrected, and was about to ascend when his friends asked him, "Lord, will you restore the kingdom now?"

And the Holy Spirit came—but that still did not mean that the time of waiting was over.

Forty-three times in the Old Testament alone, the people are commanded, "Wait. Wait on the Lord."

The last words in the Bible are about waiting: "The one who testifies to these things says, 'Surely I am coming soon.'" *It may not seem like it, but in light of eternity, it is soon. Hang on.*

A WATER-WALKER'S MOST IMPORTANT SKILL

The ability to wait well is a test of maturity. Psychologists speak of this as the ability to endure delayed gratification. M. Scott Peck writes, "Delaying gratification is a process of scheduling the pain and pleasure of life in such a way as to enhance the pleasure by meeting and experiencing the pain first and getting it over with. It is the only decent way to live."

Daniel Goleman, the author of *Emotional Intelligence*, calls the aptitude of waiting "the master aptitude."

Paul says that while we are waiting for God to set

everything right, we suffer. But suffering produces endurance; endurance, character; and character, hope. God is producing these qualities in us as we wait. Waiting is not just something we have to do while we get what we want. It is part of the process of becoming what God wants us to be.

What does it mean to wait on the Lord?

Let's start with a word about what biblical waiting is *not*. It is not a passive waiting around for something to happen that will allow you to escape your trouble. People sometimes say, "I'm just waiting on the Lord," as an excuse not to face up to reality, own up to their responsibility, or take appropriate action.

I have heard people with horrible financial habits—impulsive spending, refusal to save—in the midst of a big money mess say, "We're waiting for the Lord to provide...." This fits into the general theological category of *Don't be stupid!* Waiting on the Lord in this case does not mean sitting around hoping you get a letter from Visa that reads, "Bank error in your favor, collect $200." It probably means dragging your little financial self to a source where you can learn biblical principles for a life of good stewardship. Waiting on the Lord is a confident, disciplined, expectant, active, and sometimes painful clinging to God.

Waiting on the Lord is the continual, daily decision to say, "I will trust you, and I will obey you. Even though the circumstances of my life are not turning out the way I want them to, and may never turn out the way I would choose, I am betting everything on you. I have no plan B."

So what does it take to wait well?

PATIENT TRUST

Waiting on the Lord requires patient trust. Will I trust that God has good reasons for saying "wait"? Will I remember that things look different to God because he views things from an eternal perspective?

Peter wrote, "But do not ignore this one fact, beloved, that with the Lord one day is like a thousand years, and a thousand years are like one day. The Lord is not slow about his promise, as some think of slowness, but is patient with you, not wanting any to perish, but all to come to repentance." The story goes that an economist once read these words and got very excited.

"Lord—is it true that a thousand years for us is just like a minute to you?"

"Yes."

"Then a million dollars to us must just be a penny to you."

"Yes."

"Lord, would you give me one of those pennies?"

"All right. Wait here a minute."

There must be patient trust—trust that is willing to wait again and again day after day.

You are tempted to think, "I have been waiting long enough. I'm tired of waiting. I'm going to reach out for whatever satisfaction I can in this life and worry about the consequences later."

Maybe you have a dream about certain accomplishments—it involves your work or an area of ministry. What you hoped for is not happening—you don't know why, but you know it hurts. You are tempted to try to force it—to push, manipulate, or scheme to get what you want.

Or, perhaps you are tempted to give up ever trying to realize the potential God has given you and just drift. Will you have the patience not to force it, not to quit, but to wait patiently, to continue to learn about your giftedness, humbly receive feedback and coaching from others, grow one step at a time, and trust God's plan rather than what you think is your need?

What does it look like to wait with patient trust?

CONFIDENT HUMILITY

Waiting on the Lord also requires confident humility. The prophet said, "The effect of righteousness will be peace, and the result of righteousness, quietness and trust forever."

The result of righteousness, he discerned, will be two character qualities. The first is confidence. And this is not so much confidence in myself as confidence in the One who sustains me. It is the assurance that God is able. It entails a fearless orientation toward the future. The second quality is quietness, the opposite of arrogance and boasting, a humble recognition of my limits.

In American society there is a direct correlation between status and waiting. The higher your status, the less you have to wait. Lower-status people always wait on higher-status people.

Waiting is a good thing for people like me. It reminds me that I am not in charge. I'm the patient. I'm in the waiting room.

Prayer allows us to wait without worry. One recent night I could not sleep. I was troubled by all kinds of thoughts—"what if" kinds of thoughts. What if this doesn't change? What if something that I desperately want, I don't get? These were frantic voices. There was a semblance of truth to them—bad things can happen—but they did not lead to life.

Not long after that, I was reading the account of Jesus and his friends being in a boat, with a storm lashing them about. The disciples were quite frantic because—remember?—Jesus was sleeping.

And it struck me: There was one experience Jesus never had. He had experienced virtually every human emotion—sorrow, joy, pain. He had been tired, angry, and hopeful. But there was one thing he never experienced: He was never frantic. He never panicked. And in that moment I realized that God is never desperate.

WAITING ON THE LORD REQUIRES INEXTINGUISHABLE HOPE

Paul writes, "For in hope we were saved. Now hope that is seen is not hope. For who hopes for what is seen? But if we hope for what we do not see, we *wait* for it with patience."

Hope itself is really a form of waiting.

If you are waiting on God these days—if you are obeying him, but you don't see the results you hoped for yet—you need to know that in the Bible there is a wonderful promise attached to this waiting.

Even youths will faint and be weary,
  and the young will fall exhausted;
but those who wait for the Lord shall renew their
  strength,
   they shall mount up with wings like eagles,
  they shall run and not be weary,
   they shall walk and not faint.

Sometimes in your life you will be in an era of spiritual soaring like eagles. Maybe you are there right now. You find yourself simply borne up by God's power. You are out of the boat.

But there is another line in Isaiah's description. Sometimes we are not soaring, but we are able to run and not grow weary. If this where you are, you life isn't feeling effortless. But with persistence and determination you know you are running the race. Do not try to manufacture spiritual ecstasy. Do not compare yourself with someone who is soaring right now. Your time will come. Just keep running.

Then there is a third condition that Isaiah describes. Sometimes we will not be soaring, and we cannot run—because of doubt or pain or fatigue or failure. In those times all we can do is walk and not faint. This is not water-walking. It is just plain walking.

On D-Day an unbelievable price was paid to gain a toe-hold, a few feet of Omaha Beach in Normandy, France. It was paid in blood. At the end of D-Day, in one sense not much had changed. The vast majority of the continent of Europe was still, as it had been the day before, under the power of the swastika. There was just this one plot of ground, a few feet of sand on an obscure stretch of beach in one lonely country that was not under the domination of the enemy. The Allied forces would get a little stronger every day. There would still be a lot of fighting, a lot of suffering, a lot of dying. But now it was just a matter of time.

Until one day Paris was liberated. Then all of France. Nazi concentration camps were overrun. Prisoners were set free.

Then came V-E Day: Victory in Europe. Then V-J Day: Victory over Japan in the Pacific. The soldiers could come home.

After D-Day, V-E Day was just a matter of time. One day a woman gave birth to a son, a male child, who was destined to rule all nations with a rod of iron. He taught about and lived in a kingdom, in a kind of life that the rest of us had always dreamed of, but hardly dared hope for.

I think that sometimes in Jesus's life—as when he was on the Mount of Transfiguration—he soared. At other times—as when he faced the opposition of religious leaders—life was tougher. Yet he kept running. But when it came time to take the road to Calvary, he wasn't soaring. When the cross was placed on his bruised and bleeding back, he wasn't running. He walked. He was a young man, but he stumbled and fell that day. All he could do was get back up and walk some more.

Sometimes walking is all we can do. But in those times, walking is enough. Maybe it is when life is the hardest, when we want so badly to quit, but we say to God, "I won't quit. I'll keep putting one foot in front of the other. I'll take up my cross. I'll follow Jesus even on this road." Maybe God prizes our walking even more than our soaring and our running.

In any case, at a cost that none of us will ever fully understand, Jesus walked to Calvary. He took upon himself, on the cross, all the brokenness of the human race.

All the suffering of D-Day on Omaha Beach.

And all the suffering of all the sin and pain of every day of the history of human beings since the Fall.

After the Sabbath day, before Jesus's friends went to care for his body, the stone was dislocated—moved. In one sense nothing had changed. Pilate and the chief priests were still in charge; Caesar still reigned and didn't even know the name of this obscure Messiah in a remote country.

Nobody knew at first, except a couple of women, but that was D-Day. Now there was an opening. Tiny at first—no bigger than the entrance of a tomb.

Every time you engage in the battle, every time you resist sin, every time you proclaim the gospel, every time you give a portion of your resources for the spread of the kingdom, every time you offer a cup of cold water in Jesus's name, every time you "wait on the Lord"—every time, that opening gets a little larger. The darkness gets pushed back a little more. The light gets a little stronger.

We have some very fast runners in our world. We have some eagles that soar much higher than we can see. It is a hard thing to be a walker when you are surrounded by racers and eagles. But sometimes walking is the best we can offer God. He understands all about that. Walking counts, too.

And one day liberation will come. Make no mistake:

There will still be a lot of fighting, a lot of suffering, a lot of dying. But D-Day has already happened—when hardly anyone was looking. At the end of that one day, everything had changed. So you keep walking, because what we wait for is not more important than what happens to us while we are waiting.

Now it is just a matter of time.

And those in the boat worshiped him, saying,
"Truly you are the Son of God."
MATTHEW 14:33

HOW BIG IS
YOUR GOD?

Lord, help me to do great things as though they were
little, since I do them with your power; and little things
as though they were great, since I do them in your name.
BLAISE PASCAL

How big is your God? How big is Christ in your life?
Dale Bruner notes that right in the middle of the
story of water-walking is the word that has the power to still
the storms of fear in the troubled people of God: "Courage! I
AM! Don't be afraid!" English translations usually add a word
not found in the Greek: "I am *he*," or "It is I." But Matthew
uses the Greek version of the great, mysterious, self-revealed
name of God: "I AM WHO I AM"; "I AM has sent me to you."

Jesus intends for his fear-prone followers to understand
that this earth is in the hands of an infinite Lord whose
character and competence can be trusted. "Courage! I AM!
Don't be afraid!"

I strongly believe that the way we live is a consequence

of the size of our God. The problem many of us have is that our God is too small. When we wake up in morning, what happens if we live with a small God?

We live in a constant state of fear and anxiety because everything depends on *us*. Our mood will be governed by our circumstances.

When we have a chance to share our faith, we shrink back—what if we are rejected or cannot find the right words?

We cannot be generous because our financial security depends on us.

If we face the temptation to speak deceitful words to avoid pain, we will probably do it. If somebody gets mad at us or disapproves, we will get all twisted up in knots—we will not have the security of knowing that a giant God is watching out for us.

So how can I change my perspective?

There is a word for the process by which human beings come to perceive and declare the vastness, worthiness, and strength of God. It is called worship.

WHY DOES GOD INSIST ON WORSHIP?

Have you ever wondered why God insists on being worshiped?

When my daughters were quite small, I would sometimes play a game with them in which I would ask, "Who's the smartest, strongest, wildest, most handsome, most charming, most attractive man in the whole world?"

They would be silent for several moments, as if giving the matter deep thought, then yell, "Santa Claus!" And then scream with laughter, as if they had just said the funniest thing in the world. As they got a little older, Santa Claus would be replaced by Big Bird, Mr. Rogers, Brad Pitt, or one of their mother's old boyfriends—whose numbers are legion. Eventually I gave up playing the game altogether.

My daughters were healthy enough to realize that you do not reinforce somebody's narcissistic ego needs by sitting around telling him how great he is.

So why does God insist on our worship? Does he really need to have a whole planet full of creatures spending vast amounts of effort and time dreaming up ways to tell him how great he is? Doesn't he already know that?

Worship is not about filling God's unmet ego needs. God has made us so that when we experience something transcendentally great, we have a need to praise it. Our experience is incomplete until we can wrap words around it. When we see the Grand Tetons for the first time, a double rainbow, or a nest of baby herons getting ready for their first flight, something in our spirits demands that we express the joy we receive.

We are to worship God, not because his ego needs it, but because without worship, our experience and enjoyment of God are not complete. We worship God not so much because he needs it, but because *we* do.

I need to worship.

I need to worship because without it I can forget that I have a Big God beside me and live in fear. I need to worship because without it I can forget his calling and begin to live in a spirit of self-preoccupation. I need to worship because without it I lose a sense of wonder and gratitude and plod through life with blinders on. I need to worship because my natural tendency is toward self-reliance and stubborn independence.

I believe it is not an accident that the story of Peter walking on the water ends the way it does. "When they got into the boat, the wind ceased. And those in the boat worshiped him, saying, 'Truly you are the Son of God.'" There is a pattern at work here that recurs repeatedly in Scripture and that needs to become part of my life as well: God reveals himself. So we reflect on what God has done and respond in worship. And our understanding of God grows.

Jesus "passes by." This passing by may show itself in a highly dramatic way—a burning bush, a pillar of fire, a walk on the water. But often it happens in ways that are easily missed—in a still small voice, through a baby in an obscure manger. God may "pass by" for you in the comforting words of a friend, or in the beauty of a spring day when the earth begins to come back to life and you realize the heavens really "are telling the glory of God."

Then sometimes it will be in the act of getting out of the boat that I see Jesus passing by and I see a God who is bigger than I had imagined.

WE REFLECT ON WHAT GOD HAS DONE

Mark's version of the water-walking story says the disciples were amazed "because their hearts were hardened." They did not yet have eyes to see that in Jesus, *God had revealed himself.*

When I stop to reflect on what God has done, I seek to soften the hardness of my heart. Instead of walking through my day with blinders on, I *notice.*

Psychologists speak of a frequent human condition they call *mindlessness.* In mindlessness my body is present, but my mind is floating off somewhere else on auto pilot. Many of us suffer from mindlessness from time to time. For some of us it has become a way of life.

Mindlessness is one of the primary things that keeps us from worship. Ironically, we live in an age that seeks to eliminate mystery, and then we miss it. We have caller ID; we can know the gender of babies before they are born; exit polls tell us who was elected before we have finished voting; TV shows reveal the secrets magicians have always kept hidden—we destroy wonder and then ache for it.

But God is way too big for the wonder-killers. So we need to reflect a while.

We pause for a moment to consider the miracle called life that causes our lungs to keep sucking in air even without our remembering to give the orders, that causes our eyes to open in the morning so that we are resurrected each new day after the mini-death of sleep. What makes this happen?

I watch, as I write these words, the pink-white blossoms of a crab apple tree on the shore before a rippling lake under an azure sky; my own private sea of Galilee. Just colors—light waves at some recognizable points on the photo-spectrum—but why do they make me so glad to be alive? Where does their beauty come from? The Lord "intended to pass them by...." A miracle, a theophany crying out, "God lives! God cares! God is unspeakably good! God is so big!" to anyone not so mindless as to totally miss them.

Sometimes we miss these miracles because we are overwhelmed. But more often in my life it happens in retrospect. I see that God was at work in some way that I did not recognize at all at the time.

WE RESPOND IN WORSHIP

Responding in worship means more than just attending worship services on a regular basis.

I suspect that when the Israelites gathered for worship, they trembled and shook along with the mountain because they had risked everything on this God—left home, food, and shelter. And he wanted to pass by.

This brings us to the matter of "fearing God."

What does it mean to fear the Lord?

This fear involves reverence and awe, a healthy recognition of who God is. It also involves a recognition of our fallenness.

But worship also reminds me that the day will come when our fallenness will be utterly healed. In that day we will fully realize the truth of the saying that "perfect love casts out fear." When we worship, we look forward to the day when fear will be as defeated and destroyed as sin, guilt, and death. Worship, therefore, in reminding us of this powerful God who is for us, becomes one of the great weapons against fear.

Dallas Willard writes,

> Holy delight and joy is the great antidote to despair and is a
> wellspring of genuine gratitude—the kind that starts at our
> toes and blasts off from our loins and diaphragm through
> the top of our head, flinging our arms and our eyes and our
> voice upward toward our good God.

It may be that such worship comes quite naturally to
you. That was not the case for me. I grew up in the Swedish
Baptist church, and Swedes are not naturally expressive,
chandelier-swinging worshipers. I had to learn to respond.

Now, in worship I use every tool at my disposal—
memory, imagination, music, Scripture, images, pictures,
and dance—to magnify God in my life. In worship I
declare that God is real. So in worship, at its heart, we
magnify God. One of the Greek words for worship begins
with the prefix *mega*, meaning large, which gets attached in
our day to everything from malls to churches. In worship I
remember again that we worship the great God, the Mega
God, the Lord of lords. In C. S. Lewis's *Prince Caspian*,
one of the children comes upon Aslan, the Christ-figure of
the Narnia stories, after a prolonged absence. "Aslan, you're
bigger," she says.

"That is because you're older, little one," answered he.

"Not because you are?"

"I am not. But every year you grow, you will find me
bigger."

So it is with us and God. This is why the story of Peter
walking on the water *must* end in worship. Worship, in a

sense, closes the loop on the whole story. Worship consolidates and expresses the disciples' new understanding of who Jesus is.

When human beings get out of the boat, they are never quite the same. Their worship is never quite the same. Their world is never quite the same. Jesus is not finished yet. He is still looking for people who will dare to trust him. He is still looking for people who will refuse to allow fear to have the final word. He is still looking for people who refuse to be deterred by failure. He is still passing by. And this is your one and only opportunity to answer his call.

This is your chance of a lifetime.

Just remember one thing: If you want to walk on the water, you've got to get out of the boat.

Sources

All italics in quotations have been added by the author and are not in the original unless otherwise noted. Scripture quotations are from the *New Revised Standard Version* unless indicated otherwise.

Chapter 1

Page 1: *Roosevelt:* Theodore Roosevelt, "Citizenship in a Republic," speech at the Sorbonne, Paris, April 23, 1910.

Page 4: *"Tormented" by the waves:* Matthew 14:24 as rendered in F. D. Bruner, *Matthew,* vol. 2, Word Biblical Commentary. Dallas: Word Books, 1985, 532.

Page 4: *Garland:* David E. Garland, *NIV Application Commentary: Mark.* Grand Rapids: Zondervan, 1996, 263.

Page 4: *"Intended to pass them by":* Mark 6:48–49.

Page 5: *"While my glory passes by":* Exodus 33:22; 34:6.

Page 5: *"The Lord is about to pass by":* 1 Kings 19:11.

Page 5: *Bruner: Matthew,* 2:533.

Page 6: *"If it is you, command me":* Matthew 14:28.

Page 10: *Jeffers:* Susan Jeffers, *Feel the Fear and Do It Anyway.* New York: Fawcett Columbine, 1987, 22.

Page 13: *"You of little faith":* Matthew 14:31.

Page 16: *"Even youths will faint":* Isaiah 40: 30–31.

CHAPTER 2

Page 19: *Dante:* Dante Alighieri, *The Divine Comedy,* "Inferno," Canto 3, 35–38.

Page 20: *Bruner:* F. D. Bruner, *Matthew,* vol. 2, Word Biblical Commentary. Dallas: Word Books, 1985, 535.

Page 21: *Thoreau:* Henry David Thoreau, *Walden,* in *The Portable Thoreau.* New York: Viking Press, 1947, 344.

Page 22: *Bailey:* Kenneth E. Bailey, *Poet and Peasant: Through Peasant's Eyes.* Grand Rapids: Wm. B. Eerdmans, 1983, 167.

Page 29: *DePree:* Max DePree, *Leadership Is an Art.* New York: Dell Books, 1990, 5.

Page 31: *"You have been trustworthy":* Matthew 25:21, 23.

CHAPTER 3

Page 33: *Buber:* Martin Buber, quoted by Gregg Levoy, *Callings: Finding and Following an Authentic Life.* New York: Harmony Books, 1997, 2.

Page 34: *Calvin and Chrysostom:* Quoted in F. D. Bruner, *Matthew,* vol. 2, Word Biblical Commentary. Dallas: Word Books, 1985, 535.

Page 35: *Ryken:* Leland Ryken, *Work and Leisure.* Portland, OR: Multnomah Press, 1987.

Page 36: *"You make springs gush forth":* Psalm 104:10, 13, 14, 24.

Page 36: *"My Father is still working":* John 5:17.

Page 36: *Minear:* Paul Minear, "Work and Vocation in Scripture," in *Work and Vocation: A Christian Discussion*, ed. John Oliver Nelson. New York: Harper Brothers, 1954, 44.

Page 36: *"The* LORD *God formed man":* Genesis 2:7.

Page 40: *Palmer:* Parker Palmer, *Let Your Life Speak*. San Francisco: Jossey-Bass, 2000, 15.

Page 40: *Buechner:* Frederich Buechner, *Wishful Thinking*. San Francisco: HarperSan Francisco, 1993, 119.

Page 40: *Miller:* Arthur Miller, *The Power of Uniqueness*, 40.

Page 40: *"In the heavens he has set a tent":* Psalm 19:4–5.

Page 42: *McFeely:* William McFeely, *Grant: A Biography*. New York: W. W. Norton, 1981, 242–43.

Page 44: *"Sober judgment":* Romans 12:3.

Page 45: *Buford:* Bob Buford, *Halftime: Changing Your Game Plan from Success to Significance*. Grand Rapids: Zondervan, 1994, 100.

Page 46: *Smith:* Gordon Smith, *In Times of Choice*. Downers Grove, IL: InterVarsity Press, 1997.

CHAPTER 4

Page 51: *Thoreau:* Henry David Thoreau, *Walden*, in *The Portable Thoreau*. New York: Viking Press, 1947, 343.

Page 52: *"Peace! Be still!":* Mark 4:39.

Page 55: *Cotter:* Jeffrey Cotter, "Witness Upmanship," *Eternity*, March 1981, 22–23.

CHAPTER 5

Page 63: *Levoy:* Gregg Levoy, *Callings: Finding and Following an Authentic Life.* New York: Crown Publishers, 1997, 253.

Page 63: *Ambrose:* Stephen Ambrose, *Undaunted Courage: Meriwether Lewis, Thomas Jefferson, and the Opening of the American West.* New York: Simon & Schuster/Touchstone, 1997.

Page 67: *"Coat of many colors":* Genesis 37:3 KJV.

Page 68: *"So they hated him even more":* Genesis 37:8.

Page 70: *"Joseph found favor":* Genesis 39:4, 6.

Page 71: *"And although she spoke to Joseph":* Genesis 39:10.

Page 72: *"One day ... she caught hold of his garment":* Genesis 39:11–12.

Page 73: *"The Lord was with Joseph":* Genesis 39:21.

Page 73: *Szymusik:* cited in Julius Segal, "Possible Interventions with Risk-Prone Individuals," in *Self-Regulating Behavior and Risk Taking,* ed. Lewis Lipsitt and Leonard Mitnick. Norwood, NJ: Ablex Publishing, 1991, 334.

Page 74: *"Tired of life":* E. Schneidman and N. Farberow, "A Psychological Approach to the Study of Suicide Notes" in *The Psychology of Suicide,* ed. E. Schneidman, N. Farberow, and R. Litman. New York: Science House, 1970, 159–64.

Page 74: *Segal:* "Possible Interventions," 334.

Page 74: *"The Lord was with Joseph":* Genesis 39:21–22.

Page 76: *"Within three days Pharaoh will lift up your head":* Genesis 40:13.

Page 76: *"Within three days Pharaoh will lift up your head—from you!":* Genesis 40:19.

Page 77: *"Even though you intended to do harm to me":* Genesis 50:20.

Page 77: *Willard:* Dallas Willard, *The Divine Conspiracy.* San Francisco: HarperSanFrancisco, 1999, 237.

CHAPTER 6

Page 79: *Thoreau:* Henry David Thoreau, journal entry, September 7, 1851.

Page 81: *Bruner:* F. D. Bruner, *Matthew,* vol. 2, Word Biblical Commentary. Dallas: Word Books, 1985, 534, including Scripture quotations.

Page 84: *Jeffers:* Susan Jeffers, *Feel the Fear and Do it Anyway.* New York: Ballantine Books, 1987.

CHAPTER 7

Page 91: *Melville:* Quoted in William McFeely, *Grant: A Biography.* New York: W. W. Norton, 1981, 485.

Page 93: *"Very much afraid of Achish king of Gath":* 1 Samuel 21:12–15.

Page 94: *"David left [Gath]":* 1 Samuel 22:1.

Page 95: *"Everyone who was in distress":* 1 Samuel 22:2.

Page 96: *"With my voice I cry to the Lord":* Psalm 142:1–2.

Page 97: *"It is enough ... take away my life":* 1 Kings 19:4.

Page 97: *"An angel bake him a cake":* See 1 Kings 19:6.

Page 97: *"You are my refuge":* Psalm 142:5.

Page 98: *"Pursue; for you shall surely overtake":* 1 Samuel 30:8.

Page 99: *Burns:* David Burns, *Feeling Good.* New
York: William Morrow, 1980, 80ff.

Page 99: *Warren:* Neil Clark Warren, *Finding the
Love of Your Life: Ten Principles for Choosing the Right
Marriage Partner.* New York: Pocket Books, 1994.

Page 100: *Palmer:* Parker Palmer, *Let Your Life
Speak.* San Francisco: Jossey-Bass, 2000. Used by
permission.

Page 102: *Art and Fear:* David Bayles and Ted Orland,
*Art and Fear: Observations on the Perils (and Rewards)
of Artmaking.* Santa Barbara: Capra Press, 1993, 29.

Page 104: *Miller:* Arthur Miller, *Death of a Salesman.*
New York: Penguin Books, 1949, 110–11.

Page 104: *"You are my refuge":* Psalm 142:5.

CHAPTER 8

Page 107: *Seligman:* Martin Seligman, *Learned
Optimism.* New York: Simon & Schuster, 1990, 16.

Page 110: *Smedes:* Lewis B. Smedes, *Standing on the
Promises.* Nashville: Thomas Nelson 1998, 28.

Page 111: *"Moses sent out twelve scouts":* See Numbers
13.

Page 111: *Seligman: Learned Optimism,* 15.

Page 112: *Goleman:* Daniel Goleman, *Emotional
Intelligence.* New York: Bantam Books, 1995, 87.

Page 113: *Lasch:* Christopher Lasch, *The True and Only
Heaven.* New York: W. W. Norton, 1991, 81.

Page 113: *"I can do all things":* Philippians 4:13.

Page 114: *"Whatever is true":* Philippians 4:8.